Dividing the Rulers

The idea of democracy has been under enormous challenge in recent years, especially since the election of many populist politicians who run on a platform of pleasing electoral winners at the expense of losers. This book argues that majority rule itself is not to blame but rather that the institutional features that stabilize majorities are responsible. Despite the popular idea that social choice instability (or "cycling") makes it impossible for majorities to make optimal decisions, Yuhui Li argues that the best aspect of democracy is not the large number of people on the winning side but the fact that the winners can be easily divided and realigned with losers in the cycling process. He shows that minorities' bargaining power depends on their ability to exploit divisions within the winning coalition and induce its members to defect, an institution-alized uncertainty that is missing in one-party authoritarian systems. The reason that some democracies lose their institutional advantage to nondemocracies is often that their institutions make it too hard for the winning coalition to divide and break down.

Using simple reasoning with the help of experimental and observa-tional data, *Dividing the Rulers* theorizes and simulates why such division within the majority is important and what kind of institutional features can help a democratic system maintain it, which is crucial in preventing an undefeatable winning coalition and the "tyranny of the majority" that may come with it. These institutional solutions point to a direction in institutional reform that not only academics but also politicians and voters should collectively pursue.

Yuhui Li earned his PhD in Political Science from the University of California, Davis.

DIVIDING THE RULERS

How Majority Cycling Saves Democracy

Yuhui Li

University of Michigan Press
Ann Arbor

First paperback edition 2025
Copyright © 2019 by Yuhui Li
All rights reserved

For questions or permissions, please contact um.press.perms@umich.edu

Published in the United States of America by the
University of Michigan Press
First published in paperback August 2025

A CIP catalog record for this book is available from the British Library.

Library of Congress Cataloging-in-Publication Data

Names: Li, Yuhui, 1976– author.
Title: Dividing the rulers : how majority cycling saves democracy / Yuhui Li.
Description: Ann Arbor : University of Michigan Press, [2019] | Includes
    bibliographical references and index.
Identifiers: LCCN 2019008978 (print) | ISBN 9780472131525 (hardcover :
    alk. paper) | ISBN 9780472125920 (ebook)
Subjects: LCSH: Majorities. | Intra-party disagreements (Political parties) |
    Opposition (Political science) | Democracy.
Classification: LCC JF1051 .L5   2019 (print) | LCC JF1051 (ebook) |
    DDC 321.8—dc23
LC record available at https://lccn.loc.gov/2019008978
LC ebook record available at https://lccn.loc.gov/2019980533

ISBN 978-0-472-04013-1 (pbk.)
DOI: https://doi.org/10.3998/mpub.11300656

Cover photo by Jay Lee.

Authorized Representative: Easy Access System Europe, Mustamäe tee 50, 10621 Tallinn,
Estonia, gpsr.requests@easproject.com

For Yang,
who believes the world is not worth saving
but whose existence proves otherwise

Preface

Politics, even in its most benign form, always creates winners and losers. A good policy for some is almost always a bad policy for others. I am not saying this in a cynical way. Obviously there are common interests a polity can and should strive for, such as the prevention of nuclear wars and famines, but that is only a small part of a government's job. Most of the decisions a government makes are about whose interests should be sacrificed (e.g., paying more taxes, suffering bankruptcy, breathing dirty air, or going to jail). And exactly because every politician in every country is more or less engaged in the business of hurting someone, giving a normatively uncontroversial evaluation to a political system is always a hard job.

However, that job needs to be done. For obvious reasons, we can't afford not knowing which political systems are better than others. And that knowledge is important not only for academics but also for members of the general public because they are the ones who can demand institutional reforms from politicians either with their votes or, in countries without elections, with their physical power.

Long before I began pursuing a political science career in the United States, I had been active in Chinese media platforms, constantly debating the choice between forms of government, especially whether the Chinese model of growth-driven authoritarianism could serve as a justifiable alternative to multiparty democracy. Those debates were not very fruitful, however, because of the scarcity of political science training in China. Even though most of the opponents to democracy failed to provide rigorous arguments and seemed to be driven entirely by a fear of the unknown, the other side, including myself, did no better homework. There was one simple question that I felt especially unequipped to answer. If democracy requires majority rule, what about minorities? In other words, on what grounds can we expect that ethnic, cultural, or economic minorities will not become victims of the "tyranny of the majority" that concerned so many early masterminds of political science (Madison 2003 [1787]; Mill 2002 [1859]; Tocqueville 2001 [1835])? And, if there is no guarantee that political winners will treat losers better in democracies than in other systems, regardless of how small the losing side is, can we really say that these are better systems?

The ambition of this book, therefore, is to find out exactly how minorities manage to survive majority rule and why they fare better in some democracies than in others. Knowing this will not only provide an effective defense of democracy in general but will also help us identify which types of democratic institutions are worth particular appreciation. At a time when the number of democracies in the world has been decreasing for years, after a century of expansion, and when people are increasingly losing confidence in their elected governments, I feel intensely motivated to discuss these questions with fellow political scientists, as well as general readers who are interested in finding better choices for political institutions. I hope I will convince pessimists that democracy per se is not failing but that certain features of certain subtypes of democratic systems need to be adjusted.

After shopping through many different schools of thought on majority-minority relationships over the years, including the integrationist arguments that focus on promoting group integration and pre-electoral coalitions and the consociational arguments that focus on mandatory power sharing, I settled on one branch of the literature that appeared to be the most appealing but underdeveloped: the beneficial cycling argument briefly made by Miller (1983) and McGann (2006). I decided to start with their general ideas, improve the vulnerable parts of their theories, and provide a more refined deductive framework with original empirical analyses. This book serves to present the end result of my research and thinking in that direction. Its main findings are regarding the source of minorities' bargaining power under majority rule, the strategic interactions between electoral winners and losers, and how they respond to different countries' institutional settings. It employs accessible language to illustrate how "cycling," once deemed an unpleasant side effect of majority rule, is actually the essential feature that makes democracy superior as a system of government compared to its alternatives and makes certain subcategories of democracies preferable to others. I demonstrate how cycling makes it possible for minorities to exploit divisions within the majority and retain bargaining power outside the winning coalition.

This book, though best categorized as a comparative politics project, differs from typical works in the literature by going beyond the positive study of political phenomena and reaching an unequivocal normative conclusion, namely, the superiority of political institutions that enhance divisions within the majority. Normally, political scientists are adept at finding interesting institutional patterns but tend to be cautious about spelling out which systems are better. This is understandable because normative statements are not strictly speaking "scientific" and falsifiable. However, I do believe it is possible to connect positive science to certain uncontroversial normative assumptions, as long as they are clearly defined, to reach useful normative conclusions, which are necessary for the real-world application of science or, in short, engineering. When engineering a car, a car company not only has to acquire the science that connects designs to their outcomes but also needs to know the subjective priorities of potential consumers. The same is true for the engineering of political institutions. We already know which electoral systems create more proportional results, but one can still ask, "So what?" If we really want our science to serve as a guide for political practitioners, we need to combine it with some normative political thinking about what is "good," much as a car manufacturer needs to know the mood of the market.

I am happy to take on that job, as I identify not only as a political scientist but also, sometimes more intensely, as a marketer of ideas. I have written nearly a hundred political commentaries; lost dozens of Chinese social network accounts due to censorship; and, believe it or not, even spent numerous nights performing politically themed stand-up comedies in Sacramento venues. I enjoy studying political science first and foremost because it is a subversive science by nature. Even when working on a journal article, I motivate myself by thinking about how it could incrementally add to the pressure to upset existing power structures and bring about institutional change. This is also what is unique about this book. It may not convince everyone, but those who find it logically convincing will also enjoy the side benefit of reaching a normative consensus on what institutional features are most favorable. For American readers especially, if you feel increasingly frightened by a governing party that has become overly unified, the institutional solutions discussed in this book will likely be of great interest.

Another feature of this book I want to mention is its accessibility. I use some game theoretical logic to illustrate the democratic bargaining process, as well as some statistical methods to make sense of the data, but none of them requires sophisticated methodological training to follow along. This is because, as you will see, the key message I try to convey in this book is quite plain and simple, discernible even to the naked eye.

I owe this book first and foremost to my decade-long mentor, friend, and coauthor Professor Matthew Shugart, who has taught me nearly everything I know about political institutions, put numerous comments on every draft of every essay or chapter I put together, and turned me from an illiterate in political science to a confident researcher. Professor James Adams and Professor Ethan Scheiner also commented on my draft chapter by chapter and played a pivotal role in encouraging me to submit it. Professors Nicholas Miller and Anthony McGann are the authors of the theories on which I have built my research, and both offered incredible thoughts about my initial research in emails despite the fact that we had never met in person. I also received important guidance from a long list of scholars at different stages of my research, including Professors Barry Naughton, Arend Lijphart, Rein Taagepera, Karen Ferree, Gerry Mackie, Mathew McCubbins, Kaare Strøm, Josephine Andrews, Branislav Slantchev, and many others. At the University of Michigan Press, my editor Elizabeth Demers and the two anonymous reviewers provided invaluable insights that helped improve the book. Last but not least, I offer special gratitude to Mr. Ming Hu for his technical help in building the experiment website.

Contents

Digital materials related to this title can be found on
the Fulcrum platform via the following citable URL:
https://doi.org/10.3998/mpub.11300656

ONE

Introduction

If democracy means "majority rule," what about minorities? Political scientists have been asking this question for centuries, since the years of Madison (2003 [1787]), Tocqueville (2001 [1835]), and Mill (2002 [1859]), but they have yet to find a straightforward answer. Regardless of the types of political games a country plays, democratic or authoritarian, there are always winners and losers. What makes us believe that when the size of a winning coalition reaches 50 percent plus one it will miraculously become amicable and refrain from imposing tyranny? What makes such collective rulers more reassuring to the ruled than a handful of dictators?

The lack of a clear and deductive answer to this question is frustrating for two reasons. First, if the tyranny of the majority cannot be ruled out, how can we, as political scientists, convince people, including ourselves, that democracy is a normatively superior political system to its alternatives? Considering that such superiority is an implicit assumption of nearly all the publications and educational programs in the discipline, our ability to support it theoretically is crucial. One could easily find statistical evidence that minority groups under majority rule fare better than those under other types of government. But statistical patterns always have outliers, sometimes a lot. For a topic as high staked as the choice of regimes, which often implies the justifications for coups and revolutions, can we really assume that a country we discuss is not an outlier? Such a lack of convincing normative arguments has become increasingly frustrating in the Trump era. We keep hearing politicians and pundits identify certain presidential behaviors as threats to democracy, which is probably right. But if you ask them what's so good about democracy, they will not be able to answer.

Second, there is certainly great variation within democracies in how their governments treat the losers of the electoral games. But scholars have yet to agree on the most important explanatory variables necessary for devising institutional solutions to help underprivileged groups. Again, numerous cross-national studies give us hints about which countries are "kinder and gentler,"[1] but they fall short of offering clear guidance to institutional designers because of the lack of a powerful deductive framework.

In this research project, I dare myself to offer a single concept that is most consequential in determining how winning coalitions treat political losers. I want it to not only explain the benign tendency of majority rule in general but also the variation within democracies. I name the variable "defection cost," which is defined by the cost incurred on those who defect from the incumbent winning coalition and form a new one. I argue that the distributive outcomes are more bearable in democracies than in other systems, and more equal in proportional parliamentary systems than in other democracies, exactly because their institutions make it less costly for their power holders to realign themselves with the opposition. The constant realignment process in democracies actually results from a previously infamous phenomenon, cycling. I argue that it is cycling that truly makes democracy a superior system because the losers in their political games can "cycle" into the winning camp without relying on exogenous shocks. The variation in minority protection within democracies is also a function of how easy it is for cycling to happen.

In order to illustrate intuitively how the defection cost affects legislators' and voters' strategies, I construct a simple voting model with only three players (implying two winners and one loser). I show that as long as the defection cost is smaller than 50 percent of the distributable benefit of a given bill, the minority player enjoys a certain bargaining power and the winning coalition can easily realign. I use an online experiment of repeated prize distribution to illustrate the strategic process behind the realignment process. I also show how the model predictions are consistent with cross-national studies that associate higher equality and better minority protection with a more fragmented winning coalition, namely, a multiparty coalition government.

---

1. This terminology is used by Lijphart (1999), and cited by many, when comparing minority protections across countries.

I further argue that, although the defection cost can be affected by a country's inherent cleavage structure, it is ultimately an institutional phenomenon. I construct a dataset of largest parties' vote share and show that majority parties around the world are almost always the result of a disproportional electoral system. With some rare exceptions, they are either manufactured (without a majority of popular votes) or, less frequently, held together by heterogeneous groups through strategic voting (indicated by either a large number of swing voters or an exceptionally restrictive system). In other words, a low defection cost, which is crucial to minorities' bargaining power, can actually be engineered by simply adopting a proportional electoral system and a parliamentary system.

You may not find the institutional recommendations made in this book to be very different from those already in the literature. The book does not dispute the mainstream empirical patterns found by other scholars regarding which systems are "kinder and gentler," but it manages to provide a more parsimonious and convincing explanation to confirm the applicability of those patterns in actual high-stakes institutional design.

This book targets some important myths in the literature. It is a long-held idea among many social choice scholars (see the long list of works summarized in Miller 1983: 738) that cycling, also known as social choice instability, is an unfavorable side effect of democracy that sometimes even makes the voting process "meaningless" (Riker 1982). Miller (1983) and McGann (2006) both offer important criticism against the idea, but fall short of picturing a deductive strategic process. The first half of the book serves to elaborate the critical role cycling plays in the democratic policy-making process, without which the electoral losers would be trapped in an equilibrium of highly unequal distributive outcomes.

I also noticed that while social choice scholars tend to warn about too much cycling party system scholars are often concerned with quite the opposite, the majority groups that are overly stubborn. Duverger (1959 [1951]), Grumm (1958), Amorim Neto and Cox (1997), and Clark and Golder (2006) all have influential pieces arguing that multipartism might not emerge even under a proportional electoral system if the country has a unidimensional social cleavage. The second half of this book targets the unidimensional argument and reveals that no winning coalition is unbreakable by studying the largest party vote shares around the world.

Before I provide more details in the next chapter regarding how to place this project in several already well-studied areas, I first use this brief introduction to overview the contents of each chapter.

Why Focus on Cycling and Multipartism

In chapter 2, I review in detail the numerous previous works that try to identify the institutional conditions necessary for the well-being of minorities, especially those in divided societies where ascriptive cleavages are salient and the risk of conflict is high.

This is a topic with little consensus between the most prominent schools. The integrationist solutions (Miller 1995; Barry 2002; Horowitz 1991; Reilly 2001) focus on encouraging multiethnic parties and cultural policies that homogenize diverse groups. The consociationalist solutions (Lijphart 1969, 1975, 1977, 1999, 2002; McGarry and O'Leary 2004, 2006a, 2006b, 2009; O'Leary 2013), based on the belief that integration between hostile groups is impossible in the short run, focus on incentives, or even constitutional requirements, for postelection coalitions between group-based politicians.

Their disagreements are significant in the way in which they lead to almost opposite choices of electoral systems. For example, Horowitz (1991) and Reilly (2001) believe that an electoral system with an absolute majority requirement, such as the alternative voting system, is preferable because it encourages multiethnic parties and cross-ethnic campaigns. Lijphart (1999, 2002) and McGarry and O'Leary (2006a, 2006b) favor proportional systems because they adequately represent minorities and are therefore necessary for the formation of any cross-ethnic grand coalitions.

It is hard to choose a side because their criticisms of each other are both reasonable. According to the consociationalist arguments, majoritarian electoral systems, including alternative voting, by definition underrepresent minorities. Politicians supported by a majority, or even plurality, group may not need a preelectoral coalition to win a majority of seats. These systems will only inflate the majority's power by denying minorities their proportional seats. However, the same criticism can be directed against the consociationalists themselves. Horowitz (2002), in his debate with Lijphart (2002), argues that minority groups, even when represented in a parliament, would not enjoy any policy-making power because majority parties do not need minorities' seats to pass legislation or maintain confidence in the government. McGarry and O'Leary's (2004) defense of consociationalism focuses on certain supermajority arrangements at the constitutional level, forbidding any single-group cabinet. But such extrademocratic measures would certainly invite all kinds of side effects such as reinforcing group identities and undermining nonethnic parties (Butenschøn 1985; Rothchild and Roeder 2005).

There is, however, one school of thought that appears more promising to me, one that focuses on the idea of crosscutting and multidimensional cleavages. It can be traced back to a long list of thinkers such as Almond (1956), Lipset (1981 [1960]), Miller (1983), and Lijphart (1985) and was first elaborated theoretically by Chandra (2005). McGann (2006) provides a most comprehensive discussion of the logical chain from proportional electoral systems combined with parliamentary systems to fragmented party systems and then from the latter to better minority protection and reconciliation. Their basic idea is that institutions and policies in divided societies should be designed to encourage cleavages within any majority group of which the minorities can take advantage. Such a solution requires neither involuntary integration of hostile groups nor voluntary concession from a majority party. In other words, groups are still free to hate each other, but the division within the majority will serve to distract the division between the majority and the minority.

As I review in detail, however, the crosscutting solutions have their own weaknesses. First, we still do not know exactly what institutions can ensure that a majority group is politically divided. Even though it is a consensus that proportional electoral systems are more likely to create fragmented party systems, most scholars agree that institutions do not provide sufficient conditions (Amorim Neto and Cox 1997; Grumm 1958; Boix 1999; Horowitz 2002). No matter how proportional an electoral system is, according to these works it will not result in a fragmented party system in a country dominated by a single cleavage.

Second, the literature of crosscutting solutions has not provided a refined causal chain from multipartism to reconciliation. Miller (1983) argues that social choice instability ensures that there are no permanent losers and therefore minorities will have an incentive to keep playing the electoral game. However, this argument seems to be more about what electoral losers can hope for than what they can get. The fact that a minority cannot rule out winning does not mean it will win in the foreseeable future. How long before the uncertainty of coalition formation can actually push the minority into a cabinet post and start affecting policy?

McGann (2006) argues that the winning coalition, when fragmented, will voluntarily offer concessions to minorities in order to prevent cycling. In other words, cycling does not have to happen in order for the minorities to start benefiting from it. The problem with this argument is that it lacks a clear casual chain between concession and stability. Even if concessions are made, minorities can still induce defections from the majority to gain even more benefits. Why would a winning coalition provide any benefits in the first place if this will not eliminate the incentives for and ability of minorities to initiate cycling?

Therefore, it is important to complete the logical chain of the crosscutting solutions to unidimensional divided societies. In the following sections I overview my key theoretical and empirical chapters.

Connecting Multipartism with Distributive Equality

Chapters 3 to 5 are devoted to a mainly social choice question: whether a fragmented winning coalition will encourage equal distribution. In chapter 3, I present a model in which three players divide a certain prize repeatedly in order to explain the bargaining power of a minority under majority rule. I show that when the cost of defection from the winning coalition is sufficiently high, it is unlikely that a minority will enter the winning coalition. As long as each coalition partner makes sure that its own share of benefits in a given bill will not exceed the costs that would be incurred by a splinter, it is free to leave the minorities with zero distributed benefits. However, when the cost of defection is lower than half the distributed benefit, there is no strategy for the majority that can ensure defection will not happen because taking one of the original winners' share will be enough to cover the defection cost. Even if the majority resists defection in the short run, it will happen eventually because for either member in the majority defecting is better than waiting for the other member to defect first. Because of the randomness of the winning coalition that results from constant realignment, equality can be achieved in the long run because winners and losers will switch sides in a rather unpredictable fashion.

In chapter 4, I employ a novel experimental method to capture the process portrayed in chapter 3. I argue that the real world inequality and redistribution data cannot help us isolate political inequality between the majority and the minority from the general inequality that often results from laissez-faire competition. In the specifically designed online voting experiment, the size of redistribution is held constant for each round of the game and for each group. The only condition that varies across groups is an artificially given defection cost. The experiment does not qualify as a direct test of the previous theoretical model because of the limitation in how much the experimental setting can simulate the modeled bargaining process, yet it offers a very intuitive portrayal of how players would behave in a distributive game.

I show that groups with higher defection costs, which simulate legislatures with single-party majorities, will distribute resources more unequally between political winners and losers than will those with lower defection costs. I also show that once defection costs are set to be really low, the voting results will be highly cyclical and winning coalitions will change frequently.

In chapter 5, I further complement the experiment by comparing the results with a series of existing empirical studies and a cross-national comparison of power alternation. I show that in countries where the government is dependent on the confidence of multiple parties, the life expectancy of the governing party is much shorter than that of those with a presidential executive or a majority governing party. I argue that the latter two types of systems represent high defection costs because voter realignment at the electorate level is necessary for any cycling to happen. This also explains the scholarly consensus that proportional parliamentary systems are empirically more pro-equality and less subject to democratic breakdowns.

Explaining the Split of a Majority

Knowing that multipartism is virtuous is not enough. One could argue that a fragmented party system, no matter how desirable it is in promoting minorities' bargaining power, is simply impossible in a country dominated by a single cleavage (Amorim Neto and Cox 1997; Horowitz 2002; Grumm 1958; Boix 1999). Chapters 6 and 7 address these possible counterarguments.

In chapter 6, I argue that a dominant majority group will always split as long as small parties are proportionally represented in the electoral system. I construct a theory from both the demand and supply sides of political parties. I argue that voters in a majority group will lose control of their politicians if there is only one dominant party that represents their group. In order to hold politicians accountable for their policy positions and valence performances, voters will demand at least two parties from the majority group, even at the expense of losing a unified voice against the minority.

At the same time, politicians from the majority group are also willing to supply more than one party in order to increase the turnover of legislative seats and high appointments. The scarcity of offices compared to the number of hopeful politicians means that low-ranking politicians will make every effort to change the status quo unless the electoral system is too restrictive for them to do so.

It is hard to test the effects of proportionality simply by comparing party fragmentation between different electoral systems. This is because, as Grumm (1958) and Boix (1999) argue, electoral systems can be endogenous to the cleavage structure of the country where they are installed. Even if there is a correlation, the multidimensionality of cleavages can be a confounding variable that determines both electoral and party systems.

In chapter 7, I conduct the test using a relatively endogeneity-free method. Inspired by Rae (1967), I first identify all the countries in which the largest parties' vote share are smaller than 0.5. These are the countries we know would lose their majority parties were the electoral systems to turn proportional. I show that most of the democracies in the world belong to this group, which suggests that majority voting blocs have a tendency to split, just as my theory in chapter 6 predicts.

Among the small number of countries that do have majority voting blocs, I further identify those whose popular vote winners alternate regularly. I argue that these countries will lose their majority voting blocs if their electoral systems become more proportional. The fact of alternation implies that their majority voting blocs are not defined ascriptively. And economic groups are by definition crosscutting for the reasons I discuss in detail in chapter 7. After these countries are excluded, there are only six countries left among the 78 qualified democracies of which we cannot argue for certain that the majority parties will cease to exist under high proportionality. However, in three of the only six countries with a non-alternating majority voting bloc, the electoral systems are all exceptionally disproportional (plurality formulas plus extremely small legislatures), which suggests that their dominant parties are very likely an institutional phenomenon. As a result, the instances of unidimensional societies that concern many scholars (Horowitz 1985; Rabushka and Shepsle 1972) are most likely institutional phenomena instead of social cleavage phenomena. Crosscutting cleavages are prevented from being openly expressed most often because electoral systems do not allow it.

In sum, it takes some very diverse methods and data to illustrate how to rely on cycling and the division within the majority to ensure the functioning of a democracy and the protection of electoral losers. Let us start with what the literature has said so far in the next chapter.

TWO

Distributive Problems under Majority Rule and the Scholarly Solutions

The scholarly works that are concerned with minorities' well-being under majority rule are massive. It is far from obvious why this additional book is necessary and how it fits into the existing ocean of theories and data analyses. In order to make sense of such a large literature, it is necessary to divide it into a few exclusive categories, each with a distinct central spirit, and discuss them separately. In this chapter, I show that all existing works belong to no more than three main schools of thought based on their different solutions to the problem of protecting minorities: the integrationist solutions, which focus on reducing the salience of group identities; the consociationalist solutions, which focus on accommodating group identities with mandatory power sharing; and the crosscutting solutions, which focus on introducing additional cleavages. I explain why I chose to develop my theory based on the crosscutting solutions and how this project serves as a further step in finding the source of minorities' bargaining power in a democratic system.

Abstracting Distributive Problems under Democracy

When modern representative democracy was first invented, one of its most important purposes, as articulated in the Declaration of Independence, was to prevent tyranny. By holding periodic elections, we can expect that those who command the military and law enforcement will think twice when they are tempted to use force against their citizens. Democracy, therefore, is first and foremost a mechanism to regulate the principal-agent relationship between the voters and the politicians. Just like any other principal-agent arrangement, a democratic government is subject to all kinds of accountability problems, as summarized by Kiewiet and McCubbins (1991: 25–27), such as the hidden action and information problem, in which the agents shirk or engage in corruption with the help of the unique information access they have; Madison's Dilemma, in which the agents use their power to oppress the principal; and collective action problems, in which a collective principal or agent fails to coordinate an optimal strategy. But besides these typical problems, there is a unique feature of democracy that makes it trickier than any other principal-agent relationship, the feature Kiewiet and McCubbins call the multiple-principal problem: because the principals in a democratic system have extremely diverse interests, an agent serving one section of the principal faithfully may be a disaster for another section. Unlike the shareholders of a public company, who mostly share the same interest in increasing profitability, the voters of a country can disagree not just on every specific policy but also on the ultimate objectives of the government.

In a corporate setting, voting in a shareholder meeting should be close to a pure "valence voting" model, which means, according to Stokes (1992), voting for candidates "by the degree to which they are linked in the public's mind with conditions or goals or symbols of which almost everyone approves or disapproves." In other words, shareholders should not vote differently unless they have different factual judgments on the quality of their management. Things may get more complicated if we take into consideration cases of insider trading or related-party transactions. But at least those should be considered exceptions instead of norms.

A national election, in contrast, is a much more complex combination of both valence and spatial voting, which means that a large number of voters vote based on zero-sum ideological issues about which they fundamentally disagree (see the numerous empirical examples in Buttice and Stone 2012; Abney et al. 2013; Adams, Merrill, and Grofman 2005; Stone and Simas 2010; Stokes 1963, 1992). Of course, the heavy weight of spatial voting in most elections does not mean that we live in a Schumpeterian world where people do not share any common interests. It may simply suggest that the preelection political process already screens out those that have extremely low valence scores. Those who anticipate losing on valence may have given up running in the first place. If a homicide convict who just got out of jail became a major candidate for office, valence voting would very likely dominate the election. So the common interest of avoiding an evil candidate still exists among voters and is being protected by the democratic process. However, not electing a criminal, though important, as verified by dictatorships around the world, is far from enough for the functioning of a democracy.

As a simple way to put it, a democracy not only needs faithful agents to serve the principal in general, but it also has to solve the problem of which sections of that principal to serve when voters disagree. The first requirement is certainly a salient academic issue considering all the typical principal-agent problems the literature has identified such as politicians' corruption, shirking, short-term orientation, power abuse, and electoral fraud. But at least we are confident that there is to date no alternative to democracy that can better tackle these problems. These phenomena should keep us alert, but they cannot serve as arguments against democracy. The second requirement, however, is even harder to reach. John Stuart Mill's (2002 [1859]: 3–4) oft-cited argument that a society's suppression of individuals can be more inescapable than that of an individual dictator may suggest that democracy could have a dangerous side. For minority groups that do not always share the preferences of the mainstream, could a "benevolent dictator" be a better choice?

A more optimistic way of getting around this problem is the Median Voter Theorem (Black 1948; Downs 1957). If we choose to believe the assumption that there exists a median voter representing moderation and justice, internal disagreement among sections of the principal may not be a problem because the policy outcome will eventually conform to that median voter in a mathematically necessary way. Those who are on one extreme of the policy spectrum may not be satisfied, but at least they can avoid the opposite extreme. However, does the assumption regarding median voters really hold? Let us explore the two aspects of this question separately.

1. Does a median voter exist?
2. When a median voter exists, is his or her preference normatively favorable?

According to the vast social choice literature (Arrow 2012 [1951]; Riker 1962; Riker and Ordeshook 1973), when the social cleavage structure is multidimensional, there may not exist an equilibrium collective choice, a phenomenon known as "cycling" or "social choice instability."

I will not repeat the social choice scholars' complicated mathematical proof but will offer an intuitive example. Imagine an electorate divided into different camps by multiple issues (foreign trade, gay marriage, tax rates, etc.), just like a pizza is sliced by two or more cuts into four or more pieces. Now assume we need the consent of a majority of the voters to form a government,[1] meaning that we need enough of those pizza slices to form a shape that is larger than a semicircle. Obviously, there is more than one combination that can achieve that circular sector. Each different combination will give us a different policy portfolio because it includes a different set of voters. And which combination will finally emerge as the winning coalition? Normally we cannot predict. If one social cleavage is much more salient than the others, it may prevent the pizza slices on the opposite side of the cleavage from forming a coalition, which makes the policy result more predictable, but having only one dominant policy disagreement is not typical in complicated human societies.

The median voter assumption obviously does not work in a multidimensional scenario because the median voter on one dimension may not be the median voter on another dimension. There is no longer any mathematical guarantee that holding the median position on all policies, or any policy, will get a politician elected. So, simply put, we just cannot predict policy outcomes based on voter preferences.

The social choice instability problem is partly remedied by the concept of "uncovered set" (Miller 1980), which refers to a set of policy combinations that any other combination outside the set cannot beat. So, even though we cannot predict the exact policy outcome, we can predict a set of possible outcomes that are acceptable at least to a significant section of the society. The discovery of this concept frees us from the cynicism that often accompanies early social choice theories like those of Arrow and Riker. However, an uncovered set still leaves voters with a great deal of uncertainty. Different ways of forming coalitions among the same voters or legislators could still result in drastically different policy outcomes. Then how do we deal with that uncertainty? Should we deal with it at all? I will come back to these questions. What we know for sure is that a median voter is not guaranteed to exist.

What about the cases in which a median voter does exist? It is certainly possible that a single cleavage could dominate a country and that the voters

---

1. This is not always true due to disproportionality in electoral systems, especially those of presidential elections, but it is close enough to most of the democracies to serve as an assumption.

would give very little weight to other policy disagreements when making their voting choices. In this case, there must exist a median voter position. But the normative implications of such a position are suspicious.

As Horowitz (1985: 347) convincingly points out, whether the equilibrium policy outcome is moderate depends on whether the voters are polarized along the salient policy dimension, which is further determined by whether the main cleavage is ascriptive. Instead of repeating his centrifugal versus centripetal models of party competition, I demonstrate the point in a more intuitive way as shown in figure 1. The horizontal axes are possible policy positions of voters while the vertical axes are the frequency of voters holding each position. The voter whose score separates a distribution into two equal areas is a median voter. It is obvious that the median voter under a polarized voter distribution is actually quite far from the middle and would demand a policy that is highly unfavorable to the minority.

When would voters be highly polarized? Based on Horowitz's logic, that happens because of two factors. First, the cleavage is ascriptive in nature, such as one based on ethnicity, religion, language, and caste, which implies that everyone has a stable and unambiguous group membership. Second, there needs to be an exogenous reason, often phrased as "primordial conflict" or "ancient hatred," that makes one group dominantly prefer discriminative measures against the other. The ascriptively divided societies under such conditions have been considered the hardest cases for democratic consolidation (Rabushka and Shepsle 1972; Reilly 2002; Lijphart 2004). If the problem of unstable social choices is more a concern of the theoretical world than an actually observable disaster, the problem of bad equilibria in divided societies has been real and devastating.

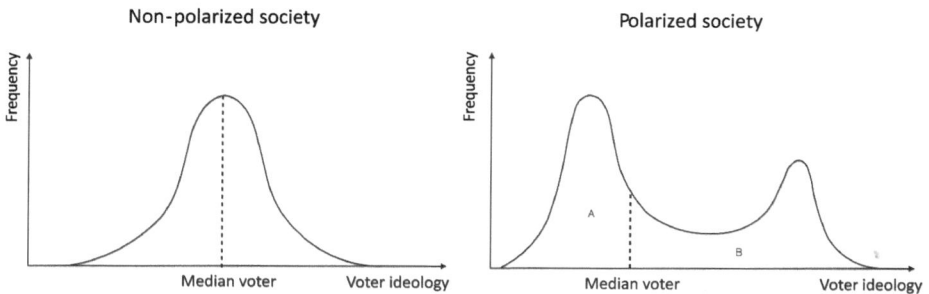

Fig. 1. Median voter positions under nonpolarized and polarized voter distributions

In general, besides holding politicians accountable, there are still two important issues we need to deal with regarding the functioning of democracy.

1. The lack of social choice stability under a multidimensional cleavage structure.
2. The extreme position of the median voter under a unidimensional cleavage structure.

Do I intend to find institutional solutions to these two problems in this book? Certainly not. In fact, the insolvability of both is logically necessary given their respective assumptions. However, this is not to say that institutional theories cannot be helpful in finding a partial remedy. Inspired by Miller (1983) and McGann (2006), I argue that there is a normative priority between these two problems. Since the first problem, as I show in detail in chapters 3–5, is far less damaging than the second, it might be a good idea to install institutions that replace the second problem with the first one, as shown in chapters 6–7. It is not a solution in a strict sense, but it can be a way to secure the lesser of the two evils.

The same tradeoff has also been repeatedly discussed in the electoral system literature, though with slightly different terminologies such as voter choices versus mandates for majority government (Powell 2000), representativeness versus preelection identifiability (Shugart and Wattenberg 2001: 29–30), highly representative government versus stable single-party government (Carey and Hix, 2011: 383), and proportionality of outcome versus ensuring stable government (Bowler, Farrell, and Pettitt 2005: 11). These scholars do not supply a definitive answer regarding which value is more important than the other partly because the answer is ambiguous for a typical nondivided society. Without any serious threat of ethnic conflict, neither a little underrepresentation of minorities nor a little postelection uncertainty appears to be urgently damaging. In a divided society, however, this tradeoff becomes vital for the reason I explain in later chapters.

In the rest of this chapter, I first review the proposed institutional cures in the literature for divided societies and explain why the crosscutting solutions are worth the most attention. I show that even though many existing works already identify and tackle the problem of unidimensionality in the right direction, they fall short of providing a deductively robust theory and a convincing test based on endogeneity-free models for the solutions they offer. And these are exactly what this book contributes.

Tackling the Distributive Problem under a Unidimensional Cleavage Structure

One of the most foundational works that explains the problem of a unidimensional cleavage structure is Donald L. Horowitz's *Ethnic Groups in Conflict* (1985). He argues that in a polarized society in which the majority and the minority are deeply divided by a single ascriptive cleavage, there tends to be a permanent majority party because each party's support base is fixed by its ascriptive identity. Since the majority group can hold on to political power safely for a long period through the control of the majority party, there is no incentive for it to make any concessions to the minority groups. Considering that even the median voter in a divided society can have intense hostility against the minority, the distributive policy of the country will follow suit and result in excessive inequality between the groups. In order to reverse such inequality, the minority group may have no choice but to resort to extrainstitutional conflict.

Fearon (1998) pushes the prediction even further and argues that the lack of institutional constraint on the majority group creates a credible commitment problem that could ultimately lead to violent secession conflict. Even if the majority has an interest in offering a deal in exchange for peace at the beginning of a conflict, its commitment would not be credible in the context of majority rule. When state power is consolidated after a peaceful period, the majority could easily renege on the deal because it would have not only the larger number votes but also the greater capability of violence at that time. Therefore, the minority always has an incentive to start fighting as early as possible in order to gain secession (or even ruling status) when there is still a chance.

These theories are very effective in explaining the numerous incidences of ethnic conflict that have occurred in transitional and even established democracies. Northern Ireland's Troubles and the sectarian violence in Iraq can be explained by the conflict between majority and minority religious factions, and the Chechen War, Yugoslav Wars, South Sudan secession, and Sri Lanka Civil War all featured one ethnic/religious majority on one side and a minority on the other. They can also explain milder but still troubling ethnic tension in countries such as Malaysia, South Africa, Guyana, and many other divided societies with a dominant majority party. Therefore, there is little disagreement in the literature that a bipolar divided society is hard to deal with. However, the prescriptions they offer are remarkably different.

O'Leary (2013: 14–30) has a most comprehensive categorization of the scholarly effort to treat a deep majority-minority divide. He finds four types of strategies in the literature: assimilation (encouraging a single national identity and cultural homogenization, prohibiting ethnic/religious parties), integration (encouraging integrated schools and multiethnic parties, single national identity in the public sphere), accommodation (recognizing cultural minorities, power sharing between groups with different identities), and disintegration (secession of individual groups). Such a typology is extremely helpful for making sense of the literature, but it is still not sufficiently exclusive and exhaustive. For example, O'Leary considers Horowitz's centripetalism as one of the subtypes of accommodation because Horowitz opposes engineering social mixing. But Horowitz's institutional solutions explicitly rely on incentivizing political parties and politicians that cultivate different ascriptive groups, about which consociationalists are pessimistic (the sharp contrast can be seen in the 2002 debate between Lijphart and Horowitz). So it is unclear how centripetalists and consociationalists can fit into one general school of thought. Another problem in O'Leary's typology is that it fails to include a newer school of thought, namely, the scholars that focus on breaking apart existing majority groups, which happens to be the focus of this book.

Therefore, I propose a slightly different approach in evaluating the literature. I group all institutional recommendations into just three categories based on only one criterion, the intermediate goal they aim to achieve.[2] The best thing about such a typology is that the categories are mutually exclusive. It is logically necessary for any institutional recommendation that a polarized society must fall into one and only one of these categories. Their pros and cons can therefore be more easily compared.

1. Integrationalist solutions: policies or institutions that try to blur the ascriptive identities of different salient groups
2. Consociationalist solutions: policies or institutions that leave the salient group identities as they are but ensure that political power will be shared by different groups
3. Crosscutting solutions: policies or institutions that try to increase the salience of within-group cleavages and break large groups into different and salient subgroups

---

2. The scholars I review in the following sections may have used different labels for themselves. For example, both Horowitz and Chandra call themselves centripetalists. But that is only a matter of terminology. What is important is which school they actually belong to according to their key intermediate variables between institutions and reconciliation.

In the following sections, I review each group of scholarly works respectively.

Integrationist Solutions

If a divided society is prone to conflict, is there any way to make it undivided? This is what integrationists have in mind when proposing their solutions. Their preferred institutions and policies all aim at one intermediate goal, reducing perceived ascriptive differences among ethnic groups. In terms of cultural policy, integrationists argue that cultural characteristics of minority groups should be restricted to the private sphere. For instance, citizens should be encouraged to learn the same official language and schools should be integrated (Miller 1995: 141–45; Barry 2002: 194–238). Political institutions could also be argued to serve the same purpose. Many scholars promote majoritarian electoral systems in order to encourage cross-ethnic coalitions and policy-centered campaigns. (Miller 1995: 151; Horowitz 1991: 180–90; Reilly 2001).

Reducing the salience of the most dangerous cleavage is certainly an intuitive reaction one would have when asked for the strategy of reconciliation between a majority and a minority. But the consociationalists' major criticism against these ideas is very hard to dismiss. Can people really forget about their salient cleavage just because they are asked to? It is true that even what appears to be ancient hatred does not have to turn into conflict if it does not coincide with political mobilization. The hard-core primordialist idea that hatred is permanent is probably an exaggeration (Eller and Coughlan 1993). However, once the conflict starts on a large scale, it is very hard for the sentiment to be simply wiped out by integration regulations.

The logic of integrated schools and public spheres may be applicable to cultural disagreement between linguistic groups. This is because language is an acquired skill and little can prevent a person from speaking two languages. Young children are especially good at learning a second language without a lot of painful effort. The nonexclusive nature of linguistic identity means that multiple groups may be able to grow more similar and even become one with the help of integrated schools and public sectors.

However, rarely is an ascriptive cleavage purely linguistic in nature. Very often it also involves different religious affiliations or broad ethnic labels such as race, tribe, and other distinguishable identities. The ethnic and religious identities are far less fluid than purely linguistic ones. Interethnic/racial/tribal marriages could certainly help blur genetic identities. But that is very unlikely to happen on a large scale in a divided society, let alone that deciding whom to marry is not something about which a government is in a position to intervene. Even if intergroup marriages were made frequent, it would take generations for a coethnic political force to emerge. In fact, even in the United States, where smaller ethnic units such as Italian or Irish communities are no longer politically salient after generations of integration, larger units like races are still a key component in political mobilization.

Religious identities, as shown in numerous historical events, are even harder to integrate than genetic ones. This is because religious beliefs, by definition, are highly exclusive. Certain artists, such as the author of the novel *Life of Pi*, may have made a subtle case for religion as a state of mind that need not be differentiated for its figurative gods. But the reality is that very few people, if any, would be a member of two different religions, or even two denominations of one religion. A child of an interracial marriage could identify with both races, but a child of an interreligious marriage, though rare, has to choose one of the parental religions.

The stability of genetic and religious identities necessarily means that the integration of different groups into one is slow if it is possible at all. In the long run, policies such as promoting integrated schools may eventually improve mutual understanding among groups, but the evidence is mixed and weak, especially when religion is involved (see research on integrated schools in Northern Ireland such as Irwin 1991; Morgan et al. 1992; McClenahan et al. 1996).

It may be argued that integration is possible as long as the incentives are strong enough. And winning legislative seats may be one of them. Reilly's (2001) study of Papua New Guinea shows that under the alternative voting system politicians often need to gain popularity among other ethnic groups in order to increase their chances to win. Even though the voters are ethnically oriented and prefer only their coethnics, they can still give their second or third preferences to a friendly politician from another group.

I agree that electoral incentives can be strong enough to induce politicians to work hard on forming coalitions and reducing within-coalition cleavages. However, such a solution is only meaningful when coalitions are needed in the first place. When a group is large enough to provide enough votes to dominate political power, why does it even care about strategic voting or electoral alliances? If Horowitz (1985) is right that a majority-minority divide is the hardest type of cleavage structure to deal with, it means that majoritarian electoral systems are only useful in relatively easy cases.

If the majority group is not interested in coalitions, can minority politicians unilaterally promote nonethnic parties in order to win votes from the majority group? They could unilaterally do so, but why would the majority politicians let them succeed easily? If a party enjoys the support of a major-ity group, it certainly has a strong incentive to emphasize or even exagger-ate the threats posed by other groups in order to avoid status quo changes. The more the groups are hostile toward each other, the safer the electoral success is for majority politicians.

In other words, assuming there is a minority in a unidimensional divided society that is not antisystem and is willing to compete electorally, there will be two contradictory incentives between the groups. The minor-ity politicians may have an incentive to blur group differences in order to win cross-group votes. The majority politicians, in contrast, always have an incentive to strengthen the hostile perception between groups to pre-vent cross-group voting. Obviously, the latter is more likely to succeed in a low-information context. This is not because the voters are biased or uneducated but is rather a joint effect of risk-aversion psychology, a cred-ible commitment problem, and the information shortcut mechanism. First, without full information on the threat level of the other group, the major-ity group may choose to prepare for the worst and assume the minority group has an evil set of mind. Its members would then play it safe by voting for their coethnics. Second, under a majoritarian electoral system, if the party representing the minority group controls the presidency or the par-liamentary majority, there is nothing that can prevent it from reneging on its electoral promises, which also deters majority voters from cross-group voting. Third, when the information costs are high, especially in countries where televisions and computers are not commonly owned, voting ethni-cally would be information efficient (see Chandra 2007). For these reasons, minority leaders cannot easily attract the majority group's votes by just unilaterally giving up an ethnic campaign.

Besides the lack of effectiveness of majoritarian electoral systems in terms of integration, it also has a serious side effect. Such systems often give a majority group a share of seats larger than its share of votes (Lijphart 1991; Reynolds 1995). Thus a majority with a small margin in terms of vote share could have a large supermajority in the legislature and be free to manipulate institutions, which would make it even harder for minorities to be heard.

In sum, even though the idea of integration is intuitively appealing, it is often not a viable solution in divided societies. Ascriptive identities, especially those overlapping with religion, are often stable and exclusive and therefore hard to make obsolete in the short run regardless of the cultural policy. The proposed majoritarian electoral systems, especially the alternative voting system, may be able to encourage cross-ethnic coalitions in countries with extremely fragmented ethnic groups such as Papua New Guinea, as Reilly (2001) shows, but they make little difference when there is a safe majority group that can win the presidency and legislative majority by itself.

Consociationalist Solutions

Consociationalism, represented by Lijphart (1969, 1975, 1977, 1985, 1999), McGarry and O'Leary (2004, 2006a, 2006b, 2009), O'Leary (2013), and Norris (2008), is so far the most influential school of thought in the literature of institutional design. Recognizing that integration is often not feasible, these scholars argue that in order for a minority to enjoy a certain level of protection in the face of a dominant majority, there needs to be a power-sharing arrangement that goes beyond normal majority rule. And that means a few specific requirements. First, a proportional electoral system is necessary to ensure a sizable block of minorities in the legislature. Second, a parliamentary system is preferred because a presidency is by definition disproportional. Third, the cabinet should be required to include both majority and minority representatives. Fourth, each group should be given the veto power to block status quo change. Fifth, in the case of a regionally concentrated minority, some form of regional autonomy, such as federalism, should be adopted.

The basic spirit of consociationalism is to recognize that the salience of ethnic hostility can be stubborn for generations and refrain from the ambition of wiping out people's unpleasant memories about each other. Instead, all of their strategies focus on forcing the representatives of these hostile groups to work together. An implicit assumption is that politicians are better at striking deals with enemies than voters are because they are more professional and have a more efficient arena for deliberation. Therefore, instead of inducing voters from different groups to vote for the same party, they accept the reality of ethnic parties but force them to form coalitions after their election.

I agree with consociationalists about the stubbornness of hostility but am unconvinced by their argument on power-sharing institutions. These solutions, though in sharp contrast with integrationist ones, face the same problem with the latter: It is unclear why a majority group with safe political power would ever respond to any power-sharing proposals. Even if the minority is proportionally represented, according to Horowitz (2002), the majority group will still enjoy a majority of seats. Why would such a dominant party ever accept a grand coalition with electoral rivals? Even if such a coalition were stipulated in the constitution, a dominant majority party would be constantly tempted to violate the constitution with the popularity it commands and the law enforcement it controls.

One way to overrule the majority is the influence from the stronger powers outside the polity. O'Leary (2004) argues that the success of the power-sharing arrangement in Northern Ireland depends greatly on the constraint imposed by the Anglo-Irish agreement in 1985. However, Northern Ireland is after all a province. If a conflict is at the national level, the outside influence is most likely minimal. In order for the United Nations or the North Atlantic Treaty Organization (NATO) to intervene in an ethnic conflict, it has to have been extremely deadly and already proliferating across the national border. So intervention at best is a postdisaster stabilizer but never a viable prevention mechanism.

Can a democracy institutionalize power sharing at the beginning of the state-building process, which often involves international assistance? It is very unlikely. The consociationalist power-sharing formula necessarily requires the definition of ethnic groups that qualify for sharing power. But before the conflict becomes escalated and salient issues become apparent, how is it possible to decide which groups should share power, considering there are many different cleavages that can divide voters (race, religion, gender, language, economic status, etc.)? Conflict is the only credible signal that can indicate which social cleavages are salient enough to be worth mandatory power sharing, which means consociationalism cannot happen before conflict. But once the conflict is in place, the majority group leaders will already have stable electoral support and no longer have any incentive to allow foreign intervention.

By the same token, power sharing between a majority and a minority, even when agreed upon, is unlikely to last. Again, unlike the Northern Ireland case, which has an outside arbitrator, any agreement between a dominant majority and a minority is hard to enforce and will result in credible commitment problems. Lijphart (1985) recognizes that "a majority segment will always be tempted to revert to majoritarian methods" even with a power-sharing agreement. However, divided societies with such a segment happen to be most in need of power-sharing agreements. Therefore, just like integrationist solutions, consociational solutions are arguably only suitable in easy cases.

Besides the feasibility problem, mandatory power sharing received other, well-justified criticisms. Butenschøn (1985) and Rothchild and Roeder (2005: 36) argue that giving a minority powers that are not earned through the electoral process is essentially undemocratic. This kind of power distribution essentially rewards the leaders of an ethnic group for the past conflict by giving them the power they would otherwise lack. It could be argued that some violent struggle is justifiable because the minority's just demand was not met. But the line is always ambiguous between a just demand and an unjust one. If political power could be won without an electoral victory, it would be rational for political leaders to invest less in elections and instead focus on issuing unreasonable demands that can lead to conflict. Leaders that are already in power would hold on to their positions and refrain from weakening group identities for fear of being "other-ised" (Wilford and Wilson 2003), meaning not belonging to any major group that is entitled to share power.

McGarry and O'Leary (2004: 33–34) counter this criticism by saying that the "pre-determination" (see Lijphart 1995 for detailed discussions) of qualified groups featured in the Northern Ireland power-sharing agreements is not intrinsic to consociationalism. They argue that such power sharing could also work between the two largest parties instead of two major groups if more fluidity is desired. In other words, the largest and second-largest parties would nominate the prime minister and deputy prime minister respectively. However, I argue that ethnic parties would be even more stable under such a system. In a normal parliamentary system, a majority coalition of small parties has the same power as a single majority party in terms of cabinet formation. In McGarry and O'Leary's hypothetical system, however, small parties can no longer affect cabinet formation even if there is no majority party. Politicians would then be very careful about forming new parties or joining smaller parties. They would stick to the two largest parties, which likely would be strongly ethnic parties in a divided society.

Of course, I am not arguing that the power-sharing arrangement in Northern Ireland is a failure. But the slowly emerging success of power sharing in the province may have resulted from the cleavage evolution that occurred prior to the agreement, to which consociationalists have not given sufficient credit. The cross-ethnic coalition was not just an artificial design, but could be a gradual consequence of an internally divided majority. And this leads us to the next subsection, regarding another group of scholars who propose to foster reconciliation by dividing the majority group.

Another important component of consociationalism is vertical power sharing through a federalist arrangement. There is little disagreement that regions with highly diverse interests should be given high levels of autonomy, which is also empirically common in large democracies (the five largest democracies by area and four of the five largest democracies by population are all federal systems). However, the effectiveness of this solution on reconciliation is often limited because it is only applicable to countries where hostile groups live in separate geographic regions. The most difficult part of ethnic conflict is exactly that groups share the same territory for historical reasons. One group may move to the traditional territory of another group through colonization, the slave trade, economic migration, urbanization, displacement by war, and so on. Under these scenarios, the autonomy or independence of a minority area often suggests that the original majority group will become a new minority group in the newly autonomous or independent territory. Majority group members' fear of becoming a minority happens to be stronger in deeply divided societies where autonomy arrangement is most seriously demanded. Therefore, regardless of the importance of federalism, it does not address the problems that arise when a majority and a minority live in the same area, and therefore it is only a partial solution.

Crosscutting Solutions

As summarized in the previous sections, integrationists focus on making voters from different groups work together to form preelection coalitions while consociationalist solutions focus on making politicians work together to form grand coalitions at the legislative and executive levels. However, both kinds of coalitions are hard to form or maintain if one group enjoys a majority of votes. In that case, the more salient the ethnic division is, the safer the majority leaders' electoral advantage is. They therefore have an incentive to prevent coalitions and employ radical ethnic propaganda.

Both Horowitz (1985) and his consociationalist opponents are right in concluding that a salient unidimensional conflict is hard to demobilize. However, this does not mean that there is nothing institutions can do in such a society. Borrowing from Madison's conclusion that "ambition must be made to counteract ambition" in Federalist Paper 51, could it be possible to introduce other cleavages into a society in order to distract attention from the existing conflict, pitting disagreement against disagreement? Almond (1956), Lipset (1981 [1960]), and Rae and Taylor (1970) were among the first modern political scientists to pay attention to the dimensionality of cleavages. Almond (1956) and Lipset (1981 [1960]: 88–89) both assert, though only in passing, that crosscutting cleavages are necessary for democratic stability. Lijphart (1985) more specifically argues that divided societies without a majority group find it easier to achieve consociational agreement because no one group can dominate the other: "A majority segment will always be tempted to revert to majoritarian method" even with a power-sharing agreement (119). One may notice that there is a subtle difference between crosscutting scenarios described by Lipset (1981 [1960]) and the no-majority scenarios described by Lijphart (1985). The former requires that a large number of voters identify themselves as members of more than one group. The latter does not require this, but it does require each group to comprise less than 50 percent of the population. Regardless of their differences, however, it is true in both scenarios that one cannot find a unified majority without salient internal agreement. So there is no need to distinguish the two terms for the sake of deriving crosscutting solutions.

Nicholas R. Miller (1983) was the first scholar to devote a whole paper to arguing for the importance of crosscutting cleavages (or, in Miller's equivalent term, "pluralistic preferences") and to unequivocally use the concept of "cycling" as a normatively favorable phenomenon. He argues that a fundamentally important requirement for democratic stability is "to induce losers to continue to play the political game, to continue to work within the system rather than to try to overthrow it." And only under a potentially cyclical cleavage structure can losers have some reasonable prospect of turning into winners regularly. This is because the distribution of political preferences tends to be highly stable (742), and the alternation of winners and losers is most often a reflection of majority cycling.

Although all these scholars recognize the importance of within-majority cleavages, they mostly consider such cleavages to be exogenously given and do not attempt to devise an institutional tool to promote them. Lijphart (1977: 42; 1985: 106) mentions briefly that an important first step in treating plural societies is to "make them more thoroughly plural" with consociational institutions (such as the Pacification of 1917 in the Netherlands), which can be considered the earliest argument to intentionally increase crosscutting cleavages.

Chandra (2007) more explicitly argues that the existence of a unidimensional cleavage structure is less an exogenous endowment than a policy failure. Using India as an example, Chandra shows that by recognizing different types of group identities in state-sponsored programs, such as job and welfare allocation and language policy, a government can actually encourage the formation of crosscutting cleavages. It may be counterintuitive to prevent ethnic conflict by making people even more divided. However, that is exactly the idea.

Based on a two-party system assumption, Chandra predicts a "centrist equilibrium" (2005: 243) in which no party has an incentive to outbid because the other party operates on other dimensions. It is not entirely accurate for Chandra to use the word *equilibrium* because what she essentially describes is an unstable condition in which a party may still outbid in the short run but would be outvoted when the other party mobilizes another cleavage dimension, but the general idea of the article is convincing: a party based on one ascriptive identity cannot secure the majority of votes by outbidding because of a cyclical preference distribution under crosscutting cleavages.

Practically speaking, however, there are two preconditions such a solution would rely on, ones that are not often satisfied in other parts of the world. First, salient crosscutting cleavages have to actually exist and be ready to be awakened, just like the Netherlands case described in Lijphart (1977) and the India case in Chandra (2007). Not in every society do ascriptive variables like religion, caste, and language crosscut each other as much as they do in India. For example, most of the Muslims in Malaysia are ethnic Malays and vice versa, and most of the Catholics in Northern Ireland identify themselves as Irish and vice versa. In fact, the castes in India in a way serve as the supraethnic and subreligious identities for mixed communities that not a lot of countries have experienced. Nonascriptive identities such as classes and industries certainly are more likely to be crosscutting. However, in the presence of a salient ascriptive cleavage, it is arguable that such cleavages are hard to invoke simply through government recognition in the absence of stronger political incentives (Horowitz 1985).

Second, such a solution relies on a government that is in favor of reconciliation and is willing to work constantly to preserve the crosscutting identities. However, if the deep reason behind ethnic conflict were exactly that it could be used by politicians to consolidate political power, why would they seriously implement the crosscutting policy that Chandra favors? If a party were able to keep winning the election with just one simple cleavage, it would certainly find every possible opportunity to emphasize that cleavage. In India, the Bharatiya Janata Party (BJP) actually has been trying to label itself as a unidimensional Hindu party. Although it may have failed to do so in the election Chandra portrays (2005: 243–45), the tactic has not become obsolete. For example, the state of Karnataka, controlled by the BJP, passed a law that prohibits cow slaughter in 2012 in the face of fierce opposition from non-Hindu minorities that depend on beef consumption and farm employment (Bureau of Democracy, Human Rights, and Labor 2014), which is obviously an outbidding strategy for securing Hindu votes.

Rothchild and Roeder's (2005) "power-dividing" theory of reconciliation bears much similarity to Chandra's logic and should also be categorized as a crosscutting solution. They argue that different government branches should be installed to create multiple majorities, none of which can be dominant, which they argue implies presidentialism and bicameralism and "non-ethnic federalism" (a federal system in which subnational units do not mirror ethnic units in order to introduce crosscutting cleavages). However, such an argument overlooks the possibility that different branches and federal units could be controlled by a single group if the cleavage is unidimensional. If there were an elected president in South Africa, for example, would the dominant party, the African National Congress (ANC), ever lose the presidential election? The same can be said about Northern Ireland and Malaysia. The dominant group is very likely to control both the legislative majority and the presidency. The reason that divided government is common in the United States is exactly that the crosscutting cleavages are already in place and dissatisfaction against a president could result in his or her party's loss in the next midterm election. But this would not be the case in a unidimensional society with a dominant ethnic cleavage. Having a presidency that is by definition disproportional means that the majority power will only be strengthened and the political inequality gap widened.

A successful crosscutting solution, therefore, should take into consideration the vulnerable parts in Chandra's (2005) and Rothchild and Roeder's (2005) arguments. First, it should be a solution that shapes political incentives at the institutional level, without relying on politicians' constant goodwill for enforcement. Second, it should not depend on the preexistence of crosscutting ascriptive cleavages. Third, it should not rely on creating different cleavages in different elections but instead should focus on creating multiple cleavages within any one election. Anthony McGann's (2006) book happens to lean in that direction.

McGann (2006: 35–85) argues that a proportional parliamentary system, as a part of what he defines as consensual democracy, is exactly what can assist the formation of a multidimensional cleavage structure. Such an institutional solution, of course, is nothing new compared to the consociationalist proposals of Lijphart and McGarry and O'Leary, which also include proportionality and parliamentarism. However, there is an important difference between the "consensual" and "consociational" institutions emphasized by the two schools of thought. In McGann's words, "Consensual democracy does not produce consensual outcomes because there are institutions that demand consensus, but as a natural outcome of majority-rule bargaining."

As previously reviewed, one of the unsolved problems for consociationalists is that they have not theorized why power sharing would even be accepted by the majority. They recognize the importance of proportionality but focus only on how it promotes minority representation in the legislature. However, the fact of minority representation does not mean that minorities have real bargaining power since the majority is normally in control of the state apparatus prior to any power-sharing bargaining. And this is exactly why consociational theories are viewed by some, such as Horowitz (2002), as only effective in places where the conflict is nearly over regardless.

The only reason for the majority to make any concession in a democratic setting has to be that the majority is divided itself, which is what McGann (2006) calls "the beauty of cycling." He argues that the importance of proportional representation, aside from representing the minority, is exactly that it ensures the expression of multidimensional cleavages in a divided society, or any society, that is threatened by an overly powerful majority. Consensual outcomes and norms in many European multiparty systems are not required by additional rules but "are a result of majority-rule bargaining in a situation where cyclical majorities are inevitable." If this is true, it is doubtful whether the consociationalist prescriptions other than proportionality and parliamentarism are still necessary, if not counterproductive. Power sharing may simply result from strategic interactions between the minority and one part of the majority based on their self-interest. Instead of forcing the coalition to consist of both groups, which has the downside of reinforcing group identities, having a voluntarily negotiated coalition conforms more closely to the principal of majority rule.

If McGann's theory (2006), as the above analyses show, has already provided a rather promising answer to the divided society problem, does this mean that the mission has been accomplished? It certainly does not. In the next section, I focus on the theoretical and empirical details that McGann has overlooked and explain why this book you are reading is necessary to make the "beauty of cycling" argument complete.

Starting from What McGann and Miller Left Out

Even though McGann's (2006) theory, which explains minorities' bargaining power using the cyclical tendency of proportional parliamentary systems, is highly inspiring and free from the vulnerabilities that characterize other institutional theories on the same issue, there are still a number of puzzles left unsolved in his rather simplified argument.

First, it is still unclear what the micromechanism between cycling and equality is. McGann considers cycling to be a deterrent against the tyranny of the majority. He argues that under a multiparty parliamentary system the winning coalition, anticipating that a disgruntled minority may persuade a part of the majority to defect, has to preemptively offer concessions to that minority. This is because the more harshly the majority treats a minority, the higher price that minority is willing to pay to induce cycling. Therefore cycling does not have to actually happen but can serve as a deterring mechanism against the tyranny of the majority.

However, there is a subtle problem that undermines such a deterrence mechanism. If we expect cycling to deter tyranny, it must be the case that the majority can prevent cycling by acting friendly. But is that the case? The tricky thing about cycling is that ANY policy outcome, equal or unequal, is subject to defeat by another (see Miller's [1983: 738] discussion of the "empty core"). Even under a completely equal distribution, a minority could still benefit from inducing defection from the winning coalition. Therefore, why should the majority make any concessions in the first place?

Table 1 is a very intuitive example, in which three players divide a certain amount of money under majority rule, that bears much resemblance to legislative bargaining without a unified majority. It is easily seen that there is simply no predictable distributive outcome. The loser in a voting game can always offer a share of his or her potential gain to another player in exchange for a defection from the current winning coalition. Any hypothetical status quo in such game (column 2 of table 1), tyrannical or not, can always be defeated by a proposal in which one of the players' benefits are taken and divided up by the other two (column 3).

Therefore, if we want to argue that there is an association between a system's cyclical tendency and equal distribution, there has to be a mechanism other than deterrence. One solution is to find answers in Miller's (1983) paper, which does not require majority concessions in order for minorities to feel satisfied. What makes cycling so important is that minorities can

TABLE 1. The Simple Proof That Any Distributive Policy among Three Players Can Be Defeated under Majority Rule by Another Policy

Player	Status Quo	Challenging Proposal	Prefer Change	Voting Outcome
A	a%	(a + c/2)%	Yes	
B	b%	(b + c/2)%	Yes	Status quo change
C	c% (c > 0)	0%	No	

Note: This table is essentially a special case of the model in McGann (2006: 72–73).

tell themselves to "wait till the next election" (743). Therefore, for Miller, cycling is less about deterrence and more about hope.

However, even though we know that cycling can give losers a hope of winning, is there any mechanism that can guarantee such a hope will materialize? What if a minority ends up on the losing side for an excessively long time? If there is no predictable equilibrium in a crosscutting context, how can we ensure that every group is equally lucky? Repeated trials of voting may eventually even up each group's luck according to the Law of Large Numbers. But how fast can the distributive outcome reach the long-term average? Miller's (1983) theory, therefore, is more about what could happen than what will happen.

Because of the these remaining puzzles left by McGann (2006) and Miller (1983), a theory with more detailed assumptions and, more important, an empirical test with more directly proximate independent and dependent variables are necessary in order to understand the microfoundations that connect cycling and equality. The next three chapters of this book, therefore, attempt to fill these gaps.

In order to deduce and test the relationship between cycling and distributive outcomes more directly, I abstract the problem into a simple three-person voting game. I first theorize, in chapter 3, how the members of such a voting body will distribute resources among themselves, building a logical link between the costs of defection from a winning coalition and minorities' bargaining power. In chapters 4 and 5, I verify this theory using both observational data and a specifically designed online voting experiment. Even though the patterns are still far from conclusive, we will have enough confidence to say that minorities enjoy better distributive outcomes when institutions make it easy for winning coalition members to defect. Consequently, countries in which the main distributive power rests in a legislative majority that depends on more than one party should be expected to serve the minority better than other systems do.

However, there is another long-standing debate that could threaten such an institutional solution: how can we ensure that a stable majority party will not emerge? McGann argues in passing that proportional parliamentary systems imply coalition governments, but is that necessarily true? In fact the electoral system literature has been vague about the issue. If we believe unidimensionality is an ascriptive phenomenon rather than an institutional one, are we really confident that a majority group will be willing to split into different parties given proportionality? Amorim Neto and Cox's (1997: 167) influential piece predicts the following, which clearly rejects institutions as sufficient conditions for party fragmentation.

A polity can tend toward bipartism either because it has a strong electoral system or because it has few cleavages. Multipartism arises as the joint product of many exploitable cleavages and a permissive electoral system.

When criticizing Lijphart's (2002) consociationalism, Horowitz (2002: 20) mentions that cross-community coalitions are often impossible because "the majority-group leaders" in "bipolar states with a majority and a minority" will not be interested in coalitions, echoing his model in Horowitz (1985). This statement also implies that majority voting blocs can be persistent even in a proportional electoral system. In addition, Grumm (1958) and Boix (1999) argue that the correlation people find between proportionality and number of parties may be subject to the endogeneity problem. It is more likely that the preexisting crosscutting cleavages caused a country to adopt a proportional system instead of the latter causing the former. One of the major themes of this book, therefore, is to find out whether a proportional electoral system is indeed powerful enough to cut through a unified majority voting block and create a set of endogenous crosscutting cleavages.

I approach this question in chapter 6 with a demand-and-supply analysis of political parties. I provide a detailed argument to show that a majority group would demand more than one party from that group for accountability reasons and that the politicians within such a group will be willing to provide more than one party in order to increase job turnover. With very few exceptions, the only obstacle to such a split is the restrictiveness of the electoral system.

How, then, do we conduct a cross-national study that avoids the endogeneity problem Grumm (1958) and Boix (1999) raise? How do we detect the causal direction in the correlation between proportionality and the lack of a majority party? In chapter 7, I adopt Rae's (1967) method for studying "manufactured majorities," but with a much larger dataset. I show that very rarely does a majority party truly earn a majority of votes. For example, in countries with more than 100 legislative seats, the United States and South Africa are the only ones in which a majority voter bloc regularly exists. And the former does not really reflect a stable ascriptive cleavage. I discuss countries with majority voter blocs case by case and show that almost no group that is as big as a national majority can avoid internal cleavages and stay unified under a proportional system.

Conclusion

I have shown in the analysis in this chapter that the existing studies addressing the equal treatment of minorities have not offered a satisfying theory. The integrationist arguments often underestimate the resilience of group identities while the consociationalists' accommodative institutions can make those identities even stronger. The schools of thought that focus on the internal divide within the majority may provide a more convincing explanation of minorities' bargaining power under majority rule. However, the logical connections and empirical support they provide are still far from perfect.

In the following chapters, I mainly target two important unsolved issues: exactly how distributive outcomes respond to social choice instability and whether that instability can be institutionally engineered.

THREE

The Inverse Relationship between Majority Unity and Minority Protection

As introduced in the previous chapters, the key motivation of this book is to identify the institutional conditions that protect the losers in electoral games, which is especially a concern in divided societies. A detailed review of the scholarly works on this matter has shown that the most convincing solution seems to be creating an internal split within the majority so that the minorities can bargain as pivotal players. However, we still lack a deductive model that can capture the microfoundations with which a majority split can affect distributive outcomes, which is the task of this chapter.

Clarifying the Normative Criterion for Distributive Policies

Before entering the world of positive theories and empirics, however, it is first necessary to have a clear definition of a normatively preferable distributive outcome. Just like designing any industrial product, designing political institutions also requires a clear understanding of a target variable. However, choosing a normatively uncontroversial distributive target is hard because the word *distribution* by definition means that different people have different preferences as to how it should be done. In this section I introduce a less controversial criterion and show why it is less subjective and more helpful for institutional design.

What kind of distributive outcomes should be considered normatively favorable? Lijphart's (1999) frequently quoted "kinder and gentler democracy" (seen in Lewin et al. 2008; Norris 2012; Armingeon 2002; Weldon and Dalton 2014) may be a natural candidate for identifying a good distributive policy. However, Lijphart does not have an unambiguous definition for this concept. Even though readers may think they know what *kindness* and *gentleness* mean in everyday dialogue, it is still hard to tell exactly what these words refer to when they are used to describe a government.

Instead of offering a definition, Lijphart (1999, 275–76) presents a list of policy outcomes he believes best reflect what a kinder and gentler democracy is supposed to entail, including better social welfare, better environmental protection, fewer prisoners and death penalties, and, in case of developed countries, more international assistance. Even though I personally sympathize with these values, none of them is free from normative controversy. Would excessive welfare hurt growth? Could the death penalty deter violent crime? Should developing countries share the costs of greenhouse gas reduction? Can international assistance really reach those in need? These are all very complicated policy questions that do not have an immediate answer. The problem of using controversial normative standards is that readers cannot be sure whether the institutions associated with these standards are truly favorable even if they are convinced by the empirical methods. For example, a fiscal conservative may want to avoid the political systems of Northern European countries exactly because they are associated with welfare states.

Even if we could find a way to support the validity of these normative claims, people in developing countries, let alone highly divided societies, would necessarily feel detached from them because of the more urgent issues these countries face. Obviously a country needs to rule out civil conflict before it can start to reduce greenhouse gasses. Then is there a more objective way to understand "kindness" and "gentleness" in a more general context?

The key source of controversy for these existing criteria is the classic tradeoff between equality and efficiency (see the summary in Okun 1977). In most western democracies, where the direction of redistribution is generally progressive (transferring resources from the rich to the poor), more equality often implies bigger government, which is associated with price distortion and deadweight losses. The criteria proposed by Lijphart, therefore, shows a leftist/liberal tendency of more redistribution and government intervention with which rightist/conservative readers may not agree.

Of course, not all redistribution hurts efficiency. The two most famous formal arguments for redistribution can be found in Pigou (1932 [1920]). First, the marginal utility (or "intensity of wants" in Pigou's words) of the poor is stronger. And therefore progressive redistribution can "increase the aggregate sum of satisfaction" regardless of the decreased sum of total wealth. Second, commodities with "externalities" (positive or negative effects on third parties besides the buyers and sellers) may be over- or undersupplied in a laissez-faire environment. Benabou's (2000) point is equally important. He argues that people with a financial constraint (the inability to borrow), especially those who are too poor to obtain an education, might not be able to invest in themselves to the socially optimal level and therefore should be subsidized. It could be argued that the distributions in western democracies mostly belong to these benevolent types. But there is no way to completely rule out the possibility of too much equality. No one can guarantee that the Northern European countries would not have grown faster had they redistributed less.

Therefore, a less controversial normative criterion must avoid such an efficiency-equality tradeoff. Consequently, I set a normative premise as follows: if a distributive policy favors political winners (those whose representatives control political power) without the justification of either equality or efficiency, such a policy should be considered discriminative. I next give some examples to clarify what that means.

One of the most intuitive examples is the distribution of national resources based on ascriptive group membership. In Northern Ireland, for example, the civil rights movement of the 1960s was partly triggered by a public housing policy that favored the already richer Protestant community (Cunningham 2001), which was by no means surprising considering that Catholics had never made it into the government. Similar but more radical policies have been in place in Sri Lanka for decades under the Sinhalese-only government. The 1956 Official Language Act, for example, effectively required fluency in Sinhala for entering public service (Sriskandarajah 2005: 344), which meant Tamils whose English was good enough for such jobs were excluded. There was also significant regional disparity in industrial investment by the state, which further exacerbated inequality between Sinhalese and Tamils in employment and financing (345). A common character of these policies is that a chunk of national resources is distributed to a group that controls the government, but that distribution is neither based on need (pro-equality) nor based on expected return (pro-efficiency).

It will be trickier if a distributive policy does channel state resources to a relatively low income group but selects the recipients based not on need but on ethnicity. Would that be considered discriminative? I argue that it depends on whether the between-group inequality is truly a dominant source of overall inequality. For example, affirmative action in India, which aims to ensure representation and employment of members of the lower castes, can be considered pro-equality and normatively acceptable because these "untouchables" were truly oppressed and significantly more disadvantaged than the rest of the society. It is hardly possible for such a policy to accidently subsidize rich individuals, at least that was true in the early years when caste discrimination was still pandemic.

However, there are also many cases in which between-group inequality was just an excuse to favor the constituencies of the governing parties. When between-group inequality is moderate compared to within-group inequality, affirmative action could even increase overall inequality by subsidizing the elite members within the moderately poorer ethnic group. In describing Fijian distributive policies, Chand (1997) states:

> The direct beneficiaries from affirmative action policies such as subsidized loans, import licenses, and tertiary study scholarships are those who can take advantage of these offerings. Often as not, these beneficiaries happen to be the educated urban elite Fijians; those who on equity considerations least deserve these privileges. For their part, the rich and educated Indians are able to finance either their own needs or work out ways to circumvent the discriminatory policies. Hence, well-intentioned affirmative actions may produce the opposite results to what is intended.

Therefore, as long as an ethnic group does not have a history of institutional discrimination enforced by the government or dominant groups, the need for ethnic-based affirmative action is doubtful. The same can be said about employment and education policies in Malaysia that are aimed at developing a Malay commercial and industrial class (Haque 2003: 248). Even though the Malay population has a lower average income than the Chinese and Indian populations, these preferential policies do not always target the poorest Malays and unnecessarily create ethnic discontent within the other groups (Crouch 2001: 227).

What if a country treats its minorities poorly but not through a distributive policy? Can we identify their discriminative feature using the same criterion? One example was mentioned in the last chapter. The BJP of India is famous for its campaign strategy, which is centered on Hindu nationalism. In some of the states the BJP governs, it banned or limited beef sales in order to please the Hindu majority, which is against cow slaughter. This seriously affected Muslims, who rely on beef as one of their major nutrition sources and on cattle farms for a large portion of their employment. The religious nationalism of the BJP is also apparent in its education policy. Many scholars (Hasan 2002; Kumar 1990; Sundar 2005) have observed that the Hindu private school network Vidya Bharati, which is often subsidized in BJP-governed states, teaches a radical anti-Islam version of history. The lack of religious tolerance in recently democratized Afghanistan is another good example. Even though people are free to choose their religion in theory, conversion from Islam to another religion is still punishable by death (Grim 2012: 23). Another nonmaterial example is the orange parades in Northern Ireland, which often enraged the Catholic minority. These parades celebrated the anniversary of the Battle of the Boyne, which forced into exile James VII and II (VII of Scotland and II of England), the last Catholic king of England, Scotland, and Ireland. On many occasions, the crowds intentionally passed through the Catholic community in a display of power (Bryan 2000; Jarman 2003), which, according to Ross (2001), could "easily become an emotionally charged, sectarian political expression." Although they were not outright government actions, the frequent occurrence of these parades more or less implied government endorsement.

It is true that in all these examples monetary redistribution is not a major issue. There is no clear flow of resources from one group to another. Can we then still use the distributive logic to make normative judgments?

I argue that, even though these discriminative policies are not monetary per se, we can still think of them in monetary terms. As in the standard practice in economics, any human preference can be measured by "utility," or "the price which a person is willing to pay for the fulfillment or satisfaction of his desire" (Marshall 1920: 78). Consequently, any policy that benefits one group, psychologically or materially, and at the same time hurts another group is essentially distributing utility between the two groups. For example, forbidding the practice of a minority religion is certainly hurting the utility of the respective religious group but increasing the comfort of fundamentalists in the majority religious groups who dislike being exposed to heresy. Such a religious ban therefore serves as a redistributive mechanism that takes religious comfort from a disadvantaged group and gives it to an already dominant religious group. The same thing can be said about language policies. Limiting the use of a local language in public schools in an area decreases the cultural autonomy of that area but increases the convenience of the members of the majority group who live in or do business there. Such a policy is essentially redistributing cultural comfort from the local group to the national majority. Similarly, the provocative parades in Northern Ireland and anti-Islam education in certain Indian schools are essentially benefiting the fundamentalists in the majority who enjoy provocation and subsequent intragroup unity while hurting minorities that are put in danger by these actions. In general, almost every salient policy dispute can be understood as a distributive issue. Whenever two groups of voters seriously disagree, it almost always means that a policy is benefiting one group, psychologically or materially, and hurting the other.

The purpose of this discussion is to find a normative standard for redistribution that does not depend on one's ideology on the left-right dimension. Compared to those implied by Lijphart (1999), the standard this study is based on is easier to reach. It does not favor welfare states but only requires that any redistribution, regardless of its magnitude, be based on either need or expected return, not on the winning status of the electoral games. Neither too much nor too little redistribution by itself is considered discriminative under such a standard as long as it is not a result of winner biases.

However, such a standard is easier said than measured. Empirically, it is hard to determine whether a redistributive policy is as pro-equality or pro-efficiency as it claims to be. In fact any bad policy can have some benefit if we look hard enough. Although the no-winner-bias standard I introduce here is less normatively controversial than Lijphart's multiple policy criteria, the downside is that it makes cross-national comparison harder because of the measurement difficulty. This is why in this and next chapter I choose to theorize and operationalize such a policy phenomenon in an abstract, three-player, zero-sum environment that is less realistic but free of confounding factors. A divide-a-dollar game by definition does not involve any laissez-faire economic activities and distributive inequality can only result from biased political decisions. This way we can easily tell which distributive outcomes are "better" than others and single out the factors that explain their differences.

What Do We Know about Distributive Outcomes under Majority Rule?

It is relatively easy to theorize distributive outcomes where a majority is perfectly unified. As I discuss in detail in later chapters, such a scenario is empirically rare even in small countries. If we observe a unified majority group, it is most likely a result of the strategic voting of several disagreeing groups. But let us come back to the causes of unidimensionality later. For the purposes of this section, all we need to know is that its effects on distributive outcomes are obvious. In a unidimensional society, political power will necessarily be controlled by a unified majority group. With no risk of losing power, it will very likely act like a dictator, though a collective one. Mill (2002 [1859]: 4) has an influential argument that such a collective dictator could be even more dangerous than a small ruling class because of the overwhelming power it possesses. Some cases of such tyranny by the majority were laid out in the last chapter.

Few would challenge my pessimism about unidimensional democratic systems, especially given the influential models of Horowitz (1985) and Rabushka and Shepsle (1972). However, what would the distributive outcomes be when there is no majority group, which is much more common in the world's democracies? This is a much trickier question, and it cannot be answered without comparing and contrasting a series of social choice models.

First of all, it needs to be clarified that the lack of a majority group does not mean the lack of a majority party. A majoritarian electoral system can easily turn a party with a minority of votes into a party with a majority of seats. Until later chapters though, we do not have to distinguish between the two phenomena. All we need to distinguish at this point is a voting body, be it an electorate or a legislature, with a stable majority and one without it. We already know the former is likely to distribute its resources in a very unequal way and now want to think about how the latter would distribute them given the same majority rule.

Theorizing the distributive outcomes in such a setting is far from easy because of the cycling phenomenon discussed in the last chapter. When a pizza is divided into more than two slices, there are many different ways to group these slices into a majority circular sector. According to Epstein (1997), the "uncovered set" approach (developed in Miller 1980) does not carry us far in narrowing down the possible outcomes, let alone rougher predictions such as the Condorcet set (Good 1971) or Pareto frontier. In a pure distributive game, the uncovered set, the set of possible voting outcomes, includes all proposals that give a majority nonzero benefits. It implies that if the number of players is three all we can predict using the uncovered set concept is that at least two players will get more than zero, which does not say much about equality among players.

By introducing stronger assumptions into the game, especially regarding the choice of an agenda setter, game theorists manage to find some more specific equilibria for pure distributive games.[1] Riker (1962), Morelli (1999), Kalandrakis (2004), and Fréchette, Kagel, and Morelli (2005) all identify equilibria that are either majoritarian or dictatorial (in the case of a strong agenda setter) in which the losers of the voting games receive little more than zero. Baron and Ferejohn (1989) find that universalistic results can emerge under certain conditions (a small number of players, high impatience, amendments allowed). Banks and Gasmi (1987) find that in a three-player committee majoritarian outcomes emerge when no more than one amendment is allowed and universalistic outcomes emerge when two amendments are allowed. Battaglini and Palfrey (2012) find from a three-player voting experiment that only in patient committees (players expecting more rounds to be played) are universalistic outcomes likely to appear (though still not as frequently as majoritarian outcomes).

In general, the literature largely agrees on the high likelihood of unequal distributive outcomes in which minorities receive a very small share, if any at all, from a given proposal under zero-sum voting games. I do not take issue with such a general prediction (in fact my own experiment in a way confirms it), but these scholars' approaches have two unsatisfying features that make them unable to answer the central puzzle of this book: how well off are minorities under majority rule?

First, none of these models and experiments predicts/tests the long-run accumulated benefits of players but only their shares in each bill. Long-run equality is certainly important because the well-being of a minority cannot be determined by one single bill. A democracy by definition involves a process of continuous voting. But the lack of long-run results in the literature is inevitable under the standard assumptions. All but two of the pieces just cited assume only one prize to be allocated. Such a setting necessarily predicts only short-run outcomes. Kalandrakis (2004) and Battaglini and Palfrey (2012) do model and test multiround distributions, but they don't report any long-term trends. This is because the highly powerful agenda setters modeled in these studies are chosen randomly at each round. This way the winners and losers by definition have to alternate frequently. Therefore, no matter how unequal each individual distributive decision is,

---

1. Note that pork barrel models by Weingast (1979) and Ferejohn, Fiorina, and McKelvey (1987) do not belong in this category. Since these articles assume a positive return of the bills voted on, the phenomena they modeled are essentially less a distributive problem than a financing problem. In fact, with a positive return guaranteed, a district does not have to depend on federal funds to invest in a project but can simply finance it through borrowing. In addition, they assume that each district proportionally takes on the burden of taxation when financing a project, which already implies a benign majority rule. Therefore, they do not answer the question of how the tyranny of the majority is prevented at the taxation stage.

the accumulated outcomes necessarily will equalize over time, which makes it pointless to calculate or report them. Therefore, unless the assumption of a random agenda setter itself can be empirically verified, these models cannot help us much in predicting long-run equality.

Second, in order to narrow the game to a solvable form, all the existing studies start their models at the voting stage when one or more agenda setters propose their bills to the whole voting body. Therefore, regardless of their subtle differences, these models share the same problem of ignoring the bargaining stage that occurs prior to voting. Such bargaining, normally conducted behind closed doors between a subset of players, is often the determinant stage of the game. In the real world, when we see two party leaders come in front of the camera to announce a coalition deal and pose for a handshaking picture, the coalition formation game is practically finished. The voting process afterward will be no more than a formality because those who vote already know what the outcome will be. While voting has to be done one at a time, bargaining talks within different subsets of players can happen at the same time. This means that the deals reached by a subset of players do not have to be constrained by the preference of an agenda setter because the latter cannot decide who negotiates with whom. Therefore, constructing a model in which everyone sits in a same room cannot realistically capture the bargaining scenario in which everyone can make proposals in any subgroup in which they participate and different subgroups are making and evaluating proposals at the same time.

Is it possible, then, to construct a model that capture such prevoting bargaining? I argue it is possible but not feasible using the theoretical tools of which I am aware. Assuming that there are three players, when each player is negotiating with two other players at the same time, the game will be extremely complicated because each player will have many different options at any given time. A player can choose to do nothing and wait for better proposals, to make his own proposal(s) to either or both rivals, to accept a proposal from one of the rivals (which essentially ends the game), or to reject a proposal from either or both rivals. And if the player decides to make a proposal, the possible shares he offers to the other players is a continuous variable, which implies an infinite number of choices. Unfortunately, such a wide range of strategic options is exactly what happens in real-world majority formation processes. Artificially reducing the options of the players may help one build a solvable model, but it is less helpful for understanding the nature of majority rule.

However, compared to the number of options, the even trickier part is the time factor. For each player, the threat that the other two players may reach a deal at any time seriously affects his ability to evaluate different proposals. He may have to accept whatever proposal he receives first just to preempt a deal between the other two players, which means he has to estimate the probability of the other players reaching a deal at any given moment.

Theoretically, we could let "nature" determine the first mover, as well as the second and third, in each single round. If nature decides that the first move is for A to make a proposal to B, then it matters greatly whether the next mover is B or C. What's more, if A is fast enough, he could make another proposal to C before B or C even moves. There is no justifiable constraint for a player to make such two moves in a row. Since the sequence of moves is essentially a random list of the three players, each of which could appear multiple times on the list, the number of branches of the game tree will be enormous.

In this chapter, therefore, I choose to offer not a full formal model but some critical fragments of a model that are just enough to put together a general picture of the players' strategies (which will be tested with an experiment in the next chapter). I have shown that "kinder and gentler" distributive outcomes are hard to identify in real politics because observed distributive inequality may result from laissez-faire competition instead of policy biases. However, what if we can construct a hypothetical scenario where 100 percent of the players' incomes are politically distributed? This is why I decide to follow the social choice literature and focus on how a three-player committee can divide a collective benefit using majority rule.

Introducing the Concept of Defection Cost

As reviewed earlier, distributive games are notoriously unpredictable because of the cyclical nature of voters' preference profiles. In a pure zero-sum prize-dividing game, all we can predict using the uncovered set method (Miller 1980) is that more than one player will get more than zero (Epstein 1997), which is hardly a prediction.

Are there any realistic constraints that can make the game more predictable? In order to restrict the voting outcomes in their multiround games, Kalandrakis (2004) and Battaglini and Palfrey (2012) stipulate that the status quo is maintained as long as the proposed bill is rejected in a given round. However, it does not create a strong enough constraint compared to the real-life voting. Under their assumptions, a randomly chosen agenda setter can always find ways to change the status quo as long as he follows a strategy similar to that illustrated in table 1. The reason for the persistence of the status quo in the actual legislative world is more than its being a default option. Even when an opposition player is given a chance to make proposals, he cannot necessarily change the status quo easily.

Therefore, if we want to theorize how voting outcomes accumulate over time, it will be helpful to introduce a concept that captures the mechanism that constrains a player's choice of partners, which I call the "defection cost." Such a concept can be abstracted from both Miller (1983) and McGann (2006), who both argue that equality in democratic systems depends on the instability of winning coalitions. The former focuses on the benefit of "pluralist preferences" (a concept similar to Chandra's [2005] "crosscutting cleavages"), while the latter advocates proportional electoral systems. But both explanatory variables converge to the same intermediate variable, the lack of a stable winning coalition. Under such a fragmented party system, defection and realignment of political forces are easier, which, according to Miller and McGann, is the key for minorities to obtain a decent share under majority rule.

I define the defection cost as the share of a total distributable benefit that a player has to pay if he switches coalition partner. Such a cost is representative to many real-world constraints on coalition formation. For example, if a legislator decides to switch parties or vote against his party leadership, he could face reputation costs or a party penalty such as the withdrawal of campaign support or even expulsion. If a party as a whole defects from a multiparty coalition, it could be viewed as unreliable or inconsistent. At the electorate level, it is also costly for voters of one party to align themselves with another party. For each individual voter, switching partisanship may not be costly, but to organize a large number of voters to do so at the same time, to the extent of breaking a winning coalition, politicians, activists, and donors will have to convey a large amount of information to the voters, acquire feedback from the voters, and adjust their platforms accordingly. Coalitions under crosscutting cleavages are not completely random exactly because of the existence of such costs.

Let us not worry about the substantive variants of this concept for the moment but only keep in mind that such a cost may be a crucial mechanism for preventing complete unpredictability in distributive games.

A Theory That Links Defection Costs to Distributive Outcomes

In this section, I try to walk through the strategic process that occurs when three players play a distributive game in a democratic setting. It is certainly a simplification compared to a real legislature, let alone a real electorate, but one cannot expect to understand more complicated actual voting and legislative processes without thinking through such a miniature version of democracy. It is especially interesting if we can predict how much the least successful player in such a game would be able to earn in the long run. Would he end up with nothing or nearly nothing? Or would the three players reach a considerable level of equality?

Besides simplicity, another benefit of using a divide-a-dollar game is that we can easily give a normative ranking to different distributive outcomes. The income of each player is purely a result of the group's political decisions unaffected by any laissez-faire market behavior or the group members' individual contributions to the economy. Therefore, the distributive outcome in such a game is purely political, meaning that any inequality in such a system has to come from a policy biased against the political losers. As was explained in detail earlier in this chapter, this kind of inequality is normatively unfavorable with little controversy because it cannot be justified on the ground of efficiency. If we can identify an institutional feature to reduce inequality in such a simple distributive game, we can safely argue that it is a good feature for political systems to have.

As the first step, I construct a hypothetical voting body with some relatively strong assumptions.

1. There are three unitary actors with equal weight in the legislature. It does not matter whether we consider them to be unified parties, factions, preelection coalitions, or simply three individuals. Each represents a third of the population in the society.
2. The actors repeatedly vote to decide how to distribute national resources among the groups they represent, which means any policy agreed on by two players will be enforced. The person who neither proposes nor accepts the final bill is considered the minority.
3. The payoff to each player consists of two parts. First, there is a reward to each player that is proportional to the benefits he earns for his group. The distribution of this reward is zero-sum because the total benefits to all the groups are constant. Second, in case a player defects from the winning coalition in the previous round and reaches a deal with the previous minority, he will have to pay a defection cost.
4. Players' agreement can only cover one round. In other words, they cannot reach an agreement regarding how to distribute resources in a future round. This is essentially a tautology

because any policies that can be covered by a single voting session should be defined as one round. Parties may be able to agree on how they will vote in a future legislative session, but under a normal system of majority rule such a commitment would not be credible. There is no third party, not even a court, that can enforce the agreement between two legislative parties to not change a policy. As a sovereign itself, a legislature can only be checked by a constitutional court or another veto player (such as a president or an upper house), but it cannot be bound by any previous agreement between any two parties.

Such a system may sound overly simple because of the small number of players. However, it does resemble a typical form of real-world legislative negotiations and can also shed light on the mechanisms of more complicated ones. In a typical nonmajoritarian legislature, even though there could be many parties, it is quite common for only the top three parties to have a pivotal impact. Parties that are too small to break a current coalition or initiate a new one cannot make a credible commitment to potential partners.

What, then, about a legislature with only two perfectly unitary players? In that case, we do not need to change the assumptions. The only reason for a majority to act like a unitary actor is the extremely high cost of defecting from that majority. Therefore, the two-actor scenario is nothing more than a special case of a three-actor scenario with a high defection cost.

Even in certain systems where negotiations regularly happen among a large number of players, the core logic should be similar. A player always has to weigh defection costs against the additional benefit new proposals will bring. Losers in coalition games will have to use either cycling or threats of cycling to earn a share for themselves. If there is any pattern that can be found in the three-player scenario between defection costs and distributive outcomes, it should at least offer some hints for more complicated scenarios.

In this hypothetical system, cycling means reducing the share of one of the winners and using what is lost to increase the shares of the new coalition. For example, a previous coalition between players A and B could give A 60 percent and B 40 percent and and leave C with nothing. In the next round, B and C could agree to divide the 60 percent of A between them and give B 70 percent and C 30 percent. But B cannot pocket 60 percent of the prize because he will have to pay a cost for having defected from the coalition with A.

Such cycling is likely to happen whenever two players can benefit from it. Let us consider three different scenarios separately: those with high, medium, and low defection costs.

(1) Low Defection Costs

Suppose a system is quite lenient toward defectors from a winning coalition. For any distributive decision reached between a defector and the original opposition, the cost incurred by the defector is less than one-third of the total benefit to be distributed. For example, if 100 dollars are distributed among the three players, anyone who decides to defect will need to pay an amount that is less than 33.3 dollars for being an unreliable political partner.

In this case, we can safely argue that there is no equilibrium strategy short of any coordination mechanism among all three players. This is because under any distributive outcome, there is always at least one winner that earns no less than one-third of the benefits. Therefore dividing up his share is always profitable for the other two players even after paying the defection cost. This conclusion does not change even if the players are completely patient. Suppose two players agree to stay loyal to their winning coalition and refuse to accept whatever lucrative proposal is made by the third player. Who is going to enforce that agreement? No matter how enthusiastic a player is about maintaining the coalition he is in, there is no way to guarantee that his partner will stay faithful. There will be a point when he decides that he can no longer trust his partner and should become the first mover before his share is divided up by the defector and the minority.

However, it is important to keep in mind that the high frequency of defection does not mean that defection must happen at every round. First, a coalition member could preempt defection by offering or accepting a proposal in which he gets much less than his coalition partner does. This is not to say that he will always do so because he would rather wait for his coalition partner to do so. It in a way depends on the player's risk-aversion profile, which I will not quantify for simplicity purposes. Second, as previously mentioned, the player who moves fastest is often consequential in such a game, which, however, is determined by "nature." So it is also possible for a player to miss the best proposal for him just because it was not offered fast enough. Therefore, without predicting exactly how frequent the defections are, what we can safely argue is that defections are highly likely.

Where there is no coordination mechanism, cycling is likely to happen constantly and membership in the winning coalition is likely to be random. Since the three players are assumed to have the same bargaining power, such a random process will be likely to give each player an equal chance of winning in the long run. In this case, therefore, there is no way for us to predict the winners and losers in any specific policy. We can only predict a long-run equality that was made necessary by the Law of Large Numbers.

Of course, the outcome may be less chaotic if coordination is an option. The three players may find it frustrating to keep cycling for two reasons. First, without any compensation in long-term benefits, cycling increases short-term risks for each player. Second, all players have to keep paying defection costs. It may be an attractive strategy for them to negotiate a long-term distributive method that is not subject to change by a simple majority so that they can still earn a third of the benefits each without paying any defection costs.

In theory they could simply give up voting in the future voluntarily and agree to divide every bit of the state resources equally among themselves, which is a much more cost-efficient way of achieving the same distributive outcome. However, such perfect agreement is not possible in the real world for many reasons. One of the most obvious difficulties is deciding exactly how much each individual will benefit from a specific policy. Even if there is agreement on who should get how much based on expected shares, there is no way to make sure the actual number will be enforced. For example, when a certain public facility is built, it is not realistic to calculate the benefit it will bring to each person in the area. Therefore, there is no way to tell whether the construction of such a facility will conform to the general agreement made at the beginning of the game. An ad hoc vote by the legislature, which is subject to the bias of the majority that happens to be in place, is still needed to decide whether the facility should be built. This necessarily means that distributive uncertainty cannot be ruled out in the real world even if policy makers prefer saving the trouble through a unanimous agreement.

The difficulties of a comprehensive agreement do not mean that there cannot be a minimalist one. The bill of rights in a typical constitutional document can be considered a distributive agreement with a minimal equality requirement. It does not stipulate exactly who gets how much, which cannot be enforced anyway, but requires that everyone must enjoy at least certain minimal benefits such as the freedom of expression, freedom from torture, freedom from arbitrary detention, property rights, and so on. It is therefore no wonder that democratic systems tend to have a

more explicit bill of rights and often a constitutional court that enforces
such rights while nondemocratic systems either fail to include these rights
in their constitutions or lack the institutional tools with which to enforce
them. This is simply because winning coalitions cycle under majority rule
and the winners need to prepare for future defections.[2]

In general, we can tell from the this analysis that when the defection
cost is in the low range (lower than a third of the distributed benefit) the
short-term outcome is highly unpredictable, just like social choice theories,
as Arrow (2012 [1951]) would predict. In the long run, however, because
of the Law of Large Numbers, each player's equal chance of entering the
coalition would translate into actual coalition membership and result
in a relatively equal distributive outcome. A coordinated supermajority
arrangement such as a constitution may help stabilize short-run outcomes
between power alternations.

(2) Medium Defection Costs

Now let us look at the scenario in which the defection cost is between
one-third and one-half of the total benefit. It is no longer so obvious that
cycling must happen. Since it is now possible for all three players to earn
less than the defection cost, dividing up the highest winner's share might
not cover the defection cost.

In the first scenario, suppose at least one of the original coalition members insists on taking a share higher than the defection cost. Then, according to the logic laid out previously, the loser can easily induce defection by
offering one of the winner's shares to the other, a share large enough to
cover the defection cost. Therefore, defection could happen.

Second, suppose that, in order to preempt defection, none of the original coalition members asks for a share higher than the defection cost,
though still higher than the minority's share. Obviously, just using one
winner's share is not enough to induce the other winner to defect. How-

---

2. One may be tempted to overinterpret these constitutional protections as a sign of the
unreliability of simple majority decisions compared to supermajority rule. However, note
that supermajority rule and simple majority rule are not mutually exclusive. A supermajority
requirement, which empowers minorities, can be exactly a strategic equilibrium under simple
majority rule simply because no one is guaranteed to stay in the majority (a more comprehensive version of such logic can be found in Buchanan and Tullock 1999). It is also important to
recognize that real-world constitutional documents are almost never made with unanimous
consent and can be biased toward the temporary majority at the time. So the supermajority
requirement to amend the constitution may be against the interest of the minority (McGann
2006).

ever, the loser still has the option of offering his own share to make up the difference. Table 2 provides an example of such a strategic choice. Suppose the defection cost is 45 percent and the two winners, A and B, each take 40 percent in the previous rounds and leave C with 20 percent. In order to induce B to defect, C can offer him 40 percent from A and 10 percent from his own share to cover the defection cost.

At first glance, such a move may seem irrational because C loses 10 percent compared to the alternative proposal. This is certainly true when players are assumed to be completely impatient and care about only the current round. However, if we go to the other extreme, where players are completely patient and care about the sum of benefits in many future rounds, the opposite is true. A proof of contradiction can easily show why doing so is actually rational. Suppose offering his own share to cover B's defection is irrational for C; then C would choose to accept the current coalition between A and B. If that is the case, A and B would enjoy a perpetual 20 percent advantage over C by staying in the coalition. Then, considering that C is completely patient, he should be willing to lose a share in the current round to trade for that perpetual advantage, which then contradicts the assumption that offering part of his own share is irrational.

Finally, there is a third possible scenario, one in which the winning coalition members simply give up their privileges in order to prevent cycling. If they expect cycling to keep happening and their expected long-term share will equalize in time anyway (given the Law of Large Numbers and the asymmetry among players), why not propose an equal distributive outcome to save the defection costs? Suppose the majority reaches a deal in which each player earns exactly one-third of the total benefit. Inducing defection in this case would not be necessary for the minority player since he would not be better off by entering the winning coalition. His expected share in case of frequent defection would still be one-third in the long run, but he would have to pay the defection cost once in a while. Therefore, no matter how patient he is, there is no point of inducing defection and entering the winning coalition.

TABLE 2. An Example of Status Quo Change under a Medium Defection Cost

Player	Partner Proposal	Challenger Proposal by C	Prefer Change?	Voting Outcome
A	40%	0	No	Defection happens (patient)
B	40%	90 to 45%	Yes	Defection does not happen (impatient)
C	20%	10%	Yes (patient)/ No (impatient)	

Given the three possible scenarios discussed above, under medium defection cost and high patience, the best strategy for a winning coalition would simply be dividing the prize among the three equally and completely eliminate the minority's incentive for inducing cycling. If the players are less patient, the winning coalition can count on the short-term incentive of the minority and worry less about defection. But they have to make sure neither of them earns more than the defection cost, which means the distributive outcome will be moderately unequal. In general, cycling should be infrequent as long as the players play rationally. And the long-run distributive outcome should be dependent on the patience of the players.

(3) High Defection Costs

By now I have shown that any defection cost that is lower than 50 percent is not likely to result in a winner-take-all outcome. Equality can result from either frequent cycling or the winners' compromise to preempt cycling (given medium defection costs and high patience). Now let us look at the scenario of high defection costs.

If the minority wants to persuade a member of the winning coalition to defect, it has to offer the latter at least a share increase that is larger than 50 percent of the total benefit. However, as long as the two winners share the benefit equally, the highest amount the minority can offer is 50 percent, lower than the amount necessary to cover the defection cost. Therefore, unlike the previous scenarios, when the defection cost is higher than 50 percent of the distributed benefit, the winners can easily prevent cycling by dividing the benefit equally. We can conclude that systems with such high defection costs are qualitatively different from the other systems because cycling is easily preventable and the minorities do not have any bargaining power.

Summing up the three scenarios, in a three-player distributive game under majority rule we should have the theoretical expectations listed in table 3.

TABLE 3. Expected Long-Run Voting Outcomes in Three-Player Distributive Games

Defection Cost	Long-Run Inequality	Cycling
Low	Low	Likely
Medium	Low	Unlikely
High	High	Unlikely

Implications of the Model

Ever since the development of Arrow Impossibility Theorem (2012 [1951]), scholars have tended to treat cycling as an undesirable feature of democracy that should be avoided whenever possible. Miller (1983: 77) reviews a long list of works, including one of his own earlier articles, that implicitly or explicitly adopt a normative premise against cycling. Even scholars, such as Mackie (2003), who cast doubt on the empirical validity of Arrow's assumptions do not dispute such a normative premise.

Miller's (1983) first attempt to reverse this normative tradition was not seriously discussed until McGann (2006) brought the topic up again in his argument in favor of proportional electoral and parliamentary systems. The theory discussed in this chapter essentially serves as a further step toward refinement and formalization of the two scholars' theories with more specific assumptions and quantitative deductions. Even though it still allows for some vagueness compared to a hard-core formal model, it offers a highly defendable logic for the favorability of institutions that allow cycling to happen.[3]

Such a simple model is certainly far from capturing real-life politics. Several strong assumptions were made for purposes of simplicity. For example, there could be more than three players in a real legislature. Each player could have different amounts of bargaining power based on the number of seats it owns. Each player might not be a unitary actor and therefore be subject to an internal split.

But even taking this into consideration, the model implies a normatively important conclusion that is robust to the removal of these assumptions: if a system imposes a high defection cost on those that break up the winning coalition, the minorities in the system will have less bargaining power and will be more likely to be marginalized. If an institutional designer is concerned with the tyranny of the majority, it should try to design the institutions in such the way that defection from the majority will not be severely punished.

What kind of system, then, is less hostile to cycling? Of course, democracy in general is more tolerant of those who switch to the opposing side of the government than authoritarian systems are. However, the defection cost is a variable even within democracies. I focus on applying this concept in real-world scenarios, especially on how they vary and their observed effects, in chapter 5.

---

3. In the appendix of the book, I discuss why a complete formalization of the divide-a-dollar-by-three game is nearly impossible, which justifies the approach I use in this chapter.

Conclusion

The word *defection* normally does not sound very pleasant, as it implies the failure of a group to achieve a collective goal. However, keep in mind that the collective goals of different groups are often contradictory. In a political setting, forming a winning coalition implies the power of forcing a group's preferences on others. Can we really sleep well if such a coalition is as unified as a pack of wolves?

By exploring the strategic dynamics of a three-player distributive game, I predict that the key source of minorities' bargaining power comes from the potential split of the winning majority. How costly it is for the members of a winning coalition to defect from that coalition makes a great difference to minorities' interests. In polities with lower defection costs, we should expect more frequent winner alternation and therefore a more equal distributive outcome. When the defection costs are as high as half the distributive benefits, cycling becomes impossible. It further implies that countries with more fragmented legislative majorities, especially those with multiparty coalition governments, can be expected to have more favorable distributive policies for minority groups.

In chapter 4, I first illustrate the three-player bargaining game with an online experiment and, in chapter 5, compare the results to those of existing empirical research.

FOUR

An Experimental Approach to Simulating the Defection Cost Effect

In the last chapter, I laid out a theory that predicts the inverse relationship between the stability of a winning coalition and the bargaining power of the opposition. When the costs for coalition members to defect are high, the winning coalition is less afraid of cycling and enjoys more freedom to make distributive decisions that disadvantage the minority groups outside the coalition. In this chapter, I simulate that process by conducting an online experiment. Just like the model in the previous chapter, the simple and isolated setting of the experiment serves to avoid normatively controversial measurements of equality or confounding variables that affect distributive outcomes.

This experiment is far from a direct test of the previous theory because of the many constraints in an experimental setting, which I discuss in detail below. But by following the interactions among players, at least we will have a very intuitive picture of how distributive outcomes evolve with coalition realignment.

The Limitations of Empirical Data

Even though the defection cost theory introduced in the last chapter is straightforward, it is hard to test empirically. When certain distributive

policies are used against minorities, it is often impossible to tell whether
the policy motives/consequences are really redistributing resources or
increasing general welfare. For example, if a minority language is removed
from the roster of official languages, one could interpret it as a distributive
policy that strengthens the power of the majority, but it could also have the
effect of reducing the translation workload. When conducting empirical
tests, it is nearly impossible to find a satisfying measurement of politically
biased distributive policies.

As was extensively discussed in chapter 2, the traditional variables used
to measure redistribution normally are not sufficiently convincing.

1. Outcome inequality measures such as the Gini coefficient.
   These measures cannot distinguish inequality caused by an
   active redistributive policy from that resulting from laissez-faire
   competition. While the latter would certainly be an interesting
   phenomenon to explain, it is not the emphasis of this study.
2. The size of redistribution such as taxation as a percentage of
   gross domestic product (GDP). These measures cannot distinguish beneficial taxes that aim to increase efficiency or equality
   from those that aim to take resources from political losers in
   order to please winners. The literature that explains the amount
   of redistribution is extensive, but the authors are all very cautious about making normative claims based on their empirical
   conclusions exactly because there is no consensus about the
   optimal level of redistribution and because it is difficult to discern the types of redistribution.

Another common way to measure a normatively controversial variable
is to survey the experts, directly coding the subjective feeling of the people
who have trustworthy knowledge about a certain country or subcountry
unit, just like the way Freedom House (2015) measures political and civil
liberty. The dataset with variables that can best proxy my dependent variable, distributive policies used against minorities, is the Minorities at Risk
Discrimination Dataset (Minorities at Risk Project 2009), which includes
the variables that measure the degree of both political and economic discrimination. However, it is hard to make cross-national comparisons using
these variables because each observation is a group instead of a country. In
order to compare different countries, one would need a formula to aggregate group-level discrimination into country-level discrimination. This
would be impossible because the criteria for including a group are not very

consistent across countries (e.g., "Taiwanese" is the majority group in Taiwan, but it was included in the data regardless). There also seems to be some face validity problems that render the interpretation of the data very difficult. For example, none of the minority groups in the United States receives "no economic discrimination" coding in the dataset, while many groups in Russia, such as the Tartars, do receive such coding. The group "Koreans" in Japan is given a lowest coding, "exclusion," which has the same value as Chechens in Russia. These controversial issues come as no surprise considering the fact that discriminative policies are hard to define even for country experts. But it does mean that I have to refrain from using these variables for cross-national tests.

In this chapter, I focus only on simulating the simple three-player model introduced in the last chapter. As argued previously, such a setting is purely distributive in nature. We do not have to worry about distinguishing different kinds of equality or different kinds of policy motives. There is only one kind of inequality, and the normative evaluation of the results is straightforward.

An Experimental Approach to Explaining Distributive Policies

In order to observe up close how the three-player committee portrayed in the previous chapter distributes resources, I adopt an experimental approach that has only been used for short-term distributive games. Although any social science experiment is at best a rough imitation of reality, its strong internal validity, despite its compromised external validity, can be a valuable addition to a literature dominated by cross-national regressions. In this section, I first introduce the setting of the experiment and then the benefits of such an experiment compared to those of cross-national studies. Finally I present the experimental results.

A key difficulty in any experimental study on rational choice is how to make sure the players play rationally. Smith and Walker (1993) show that the respondents in rational choice experiments normally converge to theoretical predictions better when the monetary rewards are higher, which is by no means surprising since people are willing to think harder and play tougher if their efforts pay. However, no matter how much money an experimenter can offer, the stakes in an experimental setting can never be as high as they are in the real world, especially when it comes to policy decisions.

Of course, if the only problem is the failure of players to play hard, the deviations from rational behavior should be random, which means, albeit with a wider confidence interval, the results shouldn't be biased. However, there is a deeper problem in testing the specific question I explore. As many scholars (Rabin 1993; Camerer 2003: chap. 3; Loewenstein et al. 1989) argue, when an experiment involves more than one person distributing resources, the sense for fairness and reciprocity can outweigh rationality. In other words, the deviation from best strategies is not just a cognitive phenomenon but can also be a moral phenomenon. For example, one of the most classic experiments concerns the ultimatum bargaining game, in which one person offers a way to split a certain prize and the other person either accepts what he is offered or rejects it and forgo the prize for both. The rational strategy for the first person is certainly to give the other side only "a crumb of the cake" (Güth and Tietz 1990: 419). And the second person will have no choice but to accept the crumb. The actual experiments, however, never turn out as predicted. The second person normally opts not to accept the crumb, and the first person, either expecting that or simply feeling guilty about getting everything, tends to split the prize more evenly than predicted.

One easy way to deal with such results is to simply amend the theory to fit the data, arguing that people are sympathetic and reciprocal. However, can we really trust the "fair" results if what we are really interested in is the high-stakes scenarios? When the money to be split is a million dollars instead of a few, would the second person reject even the "crumb"? Would the first person still be bothered by the proposal's fairness? Therefore what really needs to be amended may be the experiment instead of the theory.

Of course, researchers are always constrained financially and can never provide as large a reward to respondents as those found in real political games. However, since what we really care about is the strength of the monetary incentives relative to the concerns of reciprocity and fairness, is there any way to keep the monetary reward unchanged but reduce players' moral concerns relative to their monetary concerns?

Johnson et al. (2002) has an inspiring way to address this issue. In addition to asking paired players to play against each other, they also ask some players to play against a computer when testing a rational choice model. In the latter scenario, obviously moral concerns should not be an issue. Even though the players still do not fully conform to the rationality predictions, they do appear much more rational than when they are playing with real people. Such a phenomenon also agrees with my personal experience in playing poker and mahjong games in my twenties. When playing with real people, I tended to play in a nice way in order to appear friendly and not too greedy. However, when playing the same games online (still with real people but without seeing their faces or knowing who they are) I tended to play in a tough way so as to win as many points (not even real money) as I could. This inspired me to build a website to allow my respondents to play online without seeing each other. The nature of this experiment determines that games between a person and a computer are impossible because there are no equilibrium strategies that can be used to program the computer players. Then online games between people who do not know or see each other would be a reasonable alternative.

Another tactic I adopted in order to give monetary concerns greater weight for players is to recruit them from a low-income country, which may deviate from the common practice of recruiting college students from the universities where the research is conducted. According to Friedman and Sunder (1994: 39), there are five main reasons for the conventional recruitment strategy.

(1) ready access to the subject pool, (2) convenience in recruiting on university campus where most of the research is carried out, (3) low opportunity cost of student subjects, (4) relatively steep learning curve, and (5) some lack of exposure to confounding external information.

However, in the internet era, the first three reasons are no longer valid. When conducting an experiment online, neither the size of the pool nor the physical distance between the respondents is a problem. The internet also allows experimenters to recruit from low-income countries, in which respondents have even lower opportunity costs than college students in high-income countries, who could easily earn about ten dollars an hour by simply delivering for restaurants. The last two reasons do not apply to this specific study either. The rules of the experiment are extremely simple, requiring little education for generations familiar with complicated online games. There has been no report by any respondent complaining about an inability to understand the rules. And since it is a pure numerical money game without any reference to the outside world, external information is not likely to confound the results.

In addition, recruiting students may have the downside of narrow external validity as warned by Cunningham, Anderson, and Murphy (1974) and Enis, Cox, and Stafford (1972). College students, because of their similar educational background and life experience, may possess a decision-making style that is different from that of the general public and therefore bias the results. Such a criticism is certainly applicable to any recruitment method. But online recruitment drawing from the general public can at least get a relatively more diverse group of respondents.

Based on this analysis, I employed a new recruitment method, using an online social network tool to employ respondents from China. Even though the typical social network websites such Facebook and Twitter are blocked in China, there is a local alternative named Weibo. Because of my weekly column and other online writings in Chinese, my Weibo account enjoyed nearly 30,000 followers at the time I started my experiment, which gave me a very convenient tool with which to market the experiment. Members of my follower pool are arguably more interested in political science than the general public. But there is no obvious reason that such a difference should affect their responses to the defection costs that I test.

Such a recruitment method therefore enjoys two major benefits. First, because of the lower income level in China,[1] the monetary incentives for respondents are more effective than for US college students. Second, because the players play in a setting that resembles a normal online competitive game and never need to face each other personally, they are less sensitive to moral concerns that may affect their strategic choices. Both factors help the experiment better imitate high-stakes scenarios in which monetary incentives often outweigh moral incentives.

The Setting of the Experiment

After reading the instructions, the players are told to log in to the experimental website at roughly the same time. They will see a web page with a large number of virtual tables and can choose one to join. Whenever a table is filled with three players, the bargaining game of that table will automatically start. The game interface is intentionally designed so that the players cannot see the others' user names and will not have an emotional preference between the other players at the table. Each table will be randomly assigned a defection cost, which can take the value of 20, 40, or 60. I explain what these numbers mean for players shortly.

---

1. Even though China is considered a middle-income country, the extreme inequality (not captured by the official data) means that very few people actually enjoy the increased average income. Only 1.76 percent of the population reaches the income threshold for paying income taxes (Lee 2015: 7). Even if we include those who underreport their income, the people whose monthly salaries are higher than 600 dollars should comprise only a very small share of the population.

Figure 2 shows virtual negotiation table that appears on each player's screen. On the lower half of the screen, a player can input his proposals on how to divide the prize of the current round. If he puts 30, 70, or 0, it means he proposes to give 30 percent, 70 percent, and none of the prize to each player respectively. He is allowed to propose any three positive numbers that add up to 100. And he can choose to make a proposal to only one other player or to both. He can always change his proposal before the round ends.

As mentioned in the last chapter, the real-world coalition or legislative bargaining often determines the results before the formal voting stage. And in that bargaining stage, there is no exclusive agenda setter. Therefore, this experiment differs from similar ones in that it allows every player to propose to every other player in any given round, which better simulates what real political parties and politicians do in preparation for floor voting. This prevents the results from being unrealistically dominated by one random agenda setter, as is often the case in pure voting experiments.

Of course, the downside of such a setting is also significant, which I did not realize until after the experiment ended. Since every player can make proposal, whether or not a player will win can be significantly affected by how fast he types the numbers or even how fast his internet connection is. In an actual bargaining process, speed is also important. A party cannot sit on a proposal for too long because the other parties may form a coalition without it. But the speed factor is not as random as in the experiment because the time scale is normally hours not seconds. In other words, the experiment is more like a fast-forward version of real negotiations. I admit that such a see-who-types-faster element can distort the results, but this is the only voting experiment I know of that endogenizes agenda setters, and it may be a helpful first step in inspiring more realistic experiments in the future.

On the upper half of the screen, a player can see the proposals made to him by the other two players. After a proposal is made, the person that receives it can choose to accept it, ignore it, or make a counterproposal. When a player accepts any proposal, that round of the game ends and the three players automatically enter the next round.

In addition to the points specified in the accepted proposals, another variable will affect players' points: defection costs. If a player was in the winning coalition in the last round (being either the proposer or the accepter of the final proposal) and changes his coalition partner in the current round, a defection cost is imposed (either 20, 40, or 60, determined randomly at the beginning of the game and remaining the same until

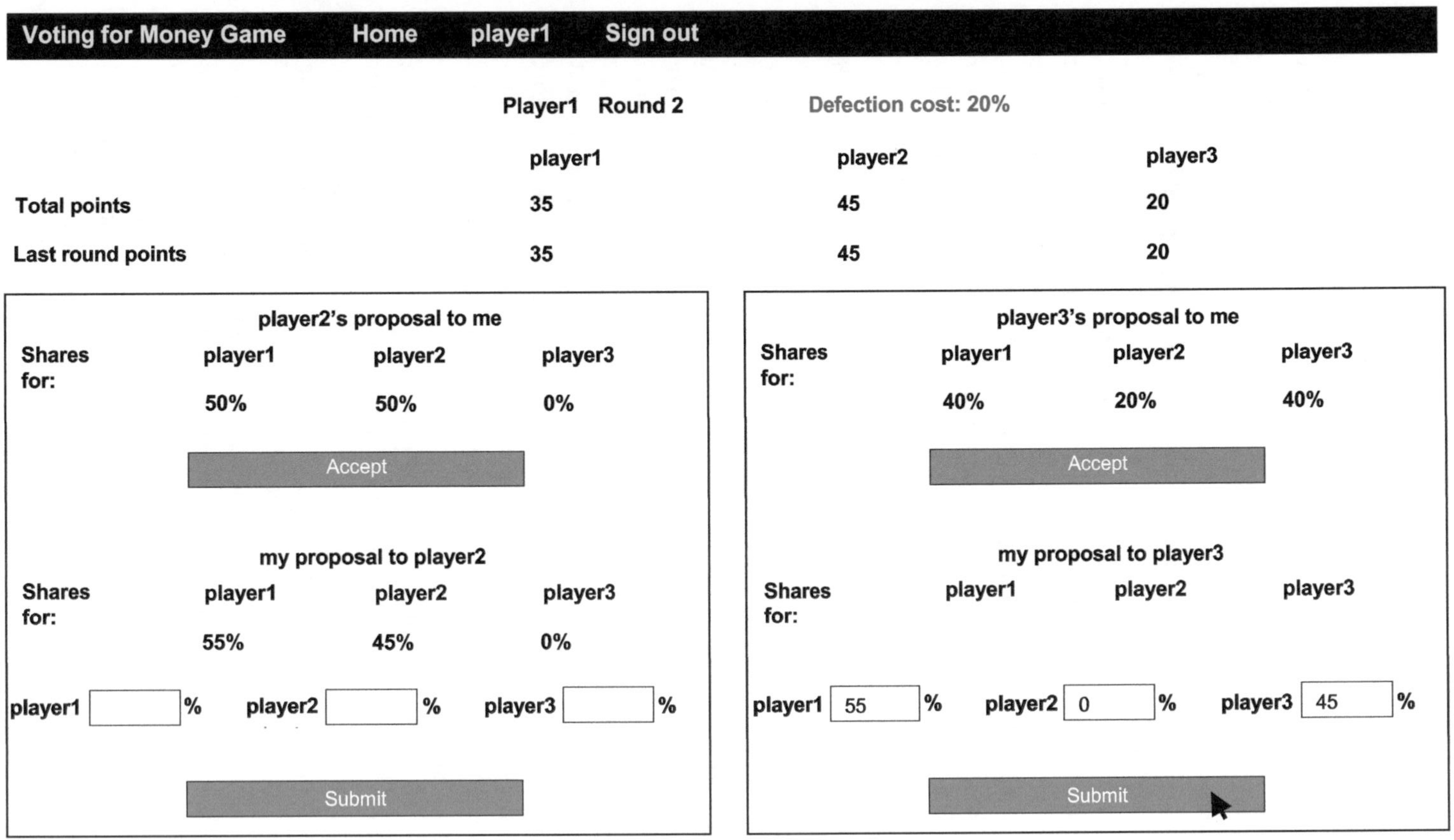

Fig. 2. The voting experiment game interface

someone switches tables). Therefore, a player's total points are calculated as his share of all the passed proposals minus the defection costs, if any, that result from changing sides.

These two types of points are essentially simulating two kinds of utilities for a legislator. The points from the proposals represent a legislator's utility in earning benefits for his constituency. The points taken as defection costs represent a legislator's costs of switching sides that are independent of his legislative achievement (discussed in detail in the last chapter). A legislator obviously has to take both into consideration when making his voting decisions.

The total prize for each round is one yuan (about 17 cents). Players are told that they can play as many rounds as they want, but only the points earned in the first 100 rounds will be counted when making the actual payment because of budget constraints. On top of the prize earned each round, there is also a show-up fee of 20 yuan for those who play more than 50 rounds. However, in order to observe long-term trends, players who switch tables more than twice in the first 50 rounds will not be paid. An ideal simulation would be designing the website in such a way that table switching is impossible, just as in real voting scenarios where players cannot switch legislatures. However, that would significantly decrease the sample size because the losing players would leave early instead of continuing at another table. The show-up fee in an experimental setting is, after all, not high enough to deter a losing player from quitting completely.

In such a setting, each player has a number of strategic tradeoffs to consider. First, he does not want to propose a share for himself that is too large because that will increase the likelihood that the other two players will reach a deal. But at the same time he does not want to be too generous when proposing because that will mean less value for him with each accepted proposal.

Second, a player also does not want to be too picky about other players' proposals to him. If he sees an acceptable proposal but fails to accept, the likelihood that the other two players will reach an agreement will be higher. But at the same time he should not accept a deal that is too harsh if he believes there is a chance of a better one.

Third, if a player reached a deal with another player in the previous round, he will need to take the defection costs into account when dealing with the third player. Similarly, if the third player wants to break an existing coalition, he also wants to provide enough incentives to cover the defection costs of the potential defector.

Experiment Results

The experiments were conducted twice in order to accumulate sufficient data. There were 184 different tables that each hosted at least one round. There were in total 2,060 proposals passed by these tables. During the experiment, the players occasionally switched tables or quit for various reasons, especially when they felt frustrated after losing. Therefore, the number of rounds played at each table by the same players varies. However, as can be seen in figure 3, there were more than 20 groups that stuck together for at least 30 rounds, which provides us with decent variation. Of course, the data for the first 15 rounds are more trustworthy because of a sample size of nearly 40.

Figure 3 also suggests that table switching happened most frequently in the first few rounds. As I show later, the distributive outcomes within each table normally equalized over time as the losing players started to realize that they could reverse their luck by inducing the defection of a winner. Consequently, table switching became less necessary.

The fact that frustrated losers were more likely to switch tables early inevitably introduced some bias into the results, which could confound their interpretation. Had they been forced to keep playing, as in real-life legislative voting, the observed long-run inequality might have been larger since the quitting decision could be endogenous to the unequal outcome at a given table. However, such a bias should not affect the comparison between tables with different defection costs. Table 4 shows the number of rounds each type of table plays on average. The differences do not appear to be statistically significant.

As mentioned at the beginning of the chapter, the key dependent variable I am concerned with is the equality of the accumulated prize among the three players. I measure it using the accumulated share of total benefits of the least successful player in each round.[2] If that share continues to be small, it suggests the existence of some "tyranny of the majority." If that

---

2. Note that this benefit measurement does not include the defection costs incurred by players. Since I consider the three players to be agents that represent three respective groups, the defection costs only apply to the agents, not their groups. Therefore it is more normatively important to look at the before-defection-costs accumulated shares because we care more about the distribution among the groups instead of their agents. Of course, one could argue that the after-defection-costs equality is also important. However, a separate analysis is not necessary because the distributive results using before-defection-costs and after-defection-costs measurements turn out to be quite similar, which is not surprising given that defections are equally likely among players and cancel each other out. I save space here by skipping the latter measurement.

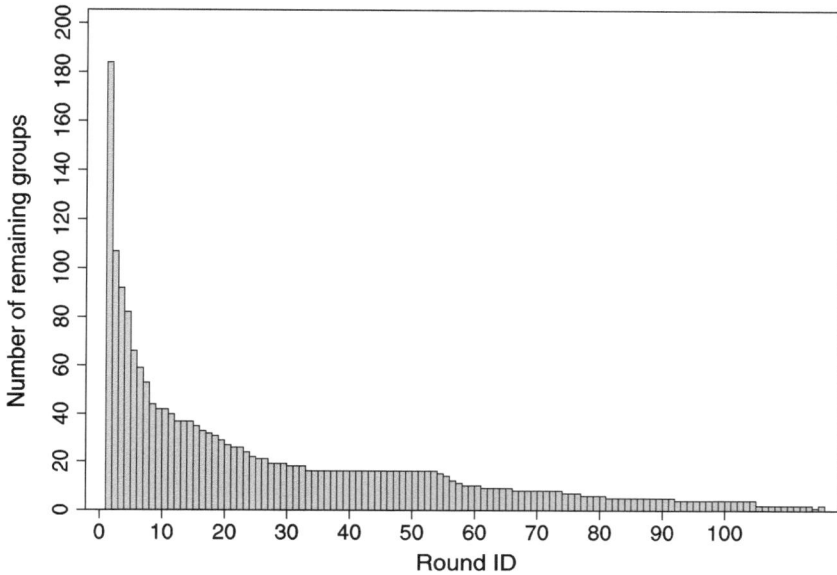

Fig. 3. Distribution of game tables according to the number of rounds played without disruption

TABLE 4. Average Number of Rounds Played at Three Types of Game Tables

Defection Cost	Average Number of Rounds Played at Each Table	Standard Error
20	18.9	4.8
40	15.7	3.7
60	18.5	5.2

Note: These numbers are based on tables that played at least two rounds. The game terminations and table switches that occurred after only one round were likely caused by mistakes or technical issues.

share reaches a number close to one-third at the end of the game, it suggests a lack of significant losers.

Before exploring the accumulated shares, however, let us first be aware of a striking short-term distributive pattern (fig. 4) in which 88.0 percent of all the passed proposals assigned zero to one of the three players. The average share of losers in all passed proposals is only 2.9 percent. This obviously means that players did not try to use equitable distribution to prevent cycling, which is supposed to happen under the medium-defection-cost scenario according to the theory laid out in the previous section. Theo-

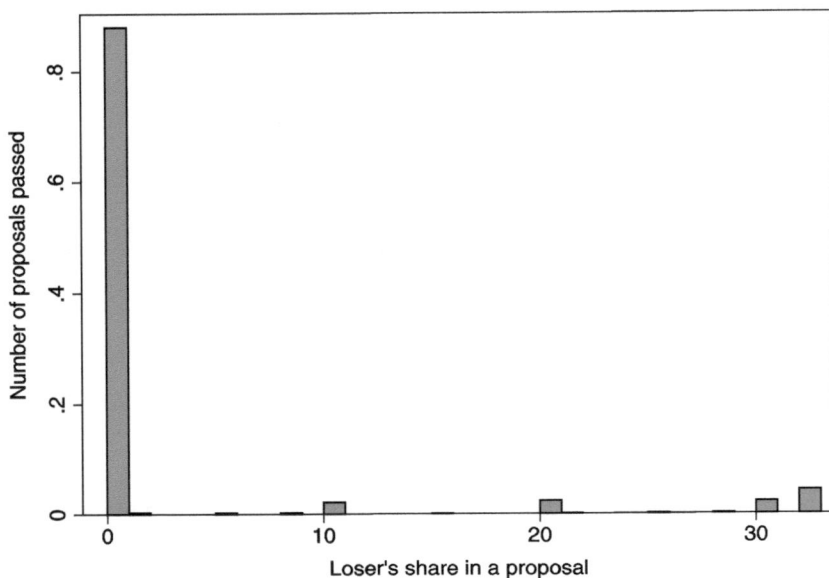

Fig. 4. Frequency distribution of all proposals based on the loser's share

retically, they could have offered the minority a share, the size of which depended on the patience of the players, in order to become free of cycling and save the defection costs (an argument also found in McGann 2006). However, the players behaved as if they were not aware of such a strategic possibility. As a result, defections were no less frequent under medium defection costs than under low defection costs.

What did the players (or the author) miss? I argue that the most likely factor preventing the medium-defection-cost tables from adopting the optimal long-run strategy was risk-taking behavior in low-stakes games (as shown in Holt and Laury 2002). Instead of employing the same strategy in every round, they may have considered the defection costs a fee required to enter the coalition gambling and enjoy that uncertainty. It may also have had to do with players' lack of time in which to engage in mathematical thinking. In fact, I myself did not realize such an optimal strategy when designing the experiment. The intensity of the bidding process during the game makes it even less likely for a player to quickly realize that no one can expect more than one-third of the benefits in the long run once cycling starts.

Note that although the players generally missed the opportunity to avoid cycling, this does not mean that they employed no strategic thinking

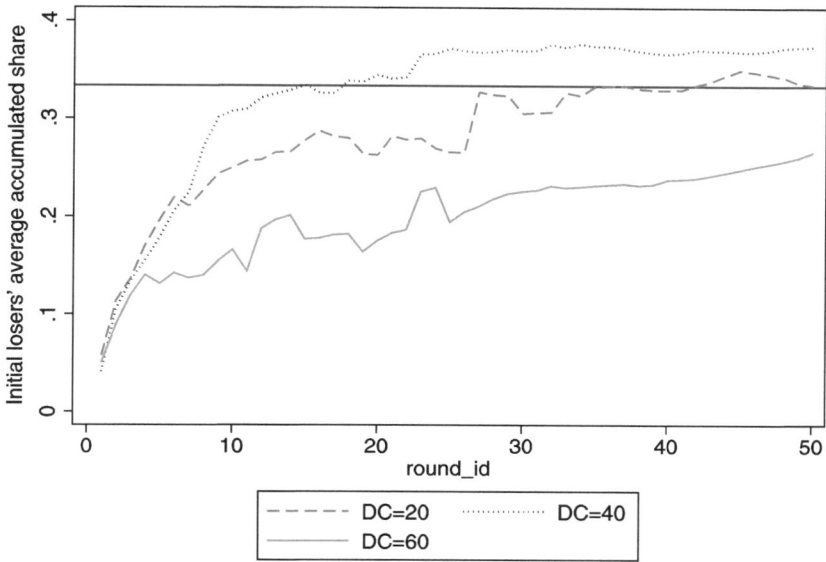

Fig. 5.Initial losers' average accumulated shares by defection costs

in the experiment. In fact, the long-run results show that average players were quite adept at using realignment to advance their interests.

First, let us compare the payoff growth of all the initial losers in the first round. Figure 5 shows their average accumulated share of the total prize under each defection cost. The horizontal axis is the number of rounds the tables have played (in other words, the number of proposals the players have passed). Obviously, the initial losers in all three groups started from a very low point. Most started from zero, as implied in figure 3 on individual proposals. A number of high-equality game tables pulled the averages slightly above zero, about 0.005. What we see in figure 5 is that these initial losers did not wait long before disturbing the existing winning coalitions. Their accumulated shares sharply increased in the first few rounds regardless of the defection costs. The initial losers in the medium-defection-cost groups seem to perform best, but those in low-defection-cost groups also caught up eventually. In both groups they eventually reached the one-third line, which means that on average they became better off than the average player in their respective groups.

The initial losers in the high-defection-cost groups had a harder time catching up, which is not surprising given the theories laid out the chapter

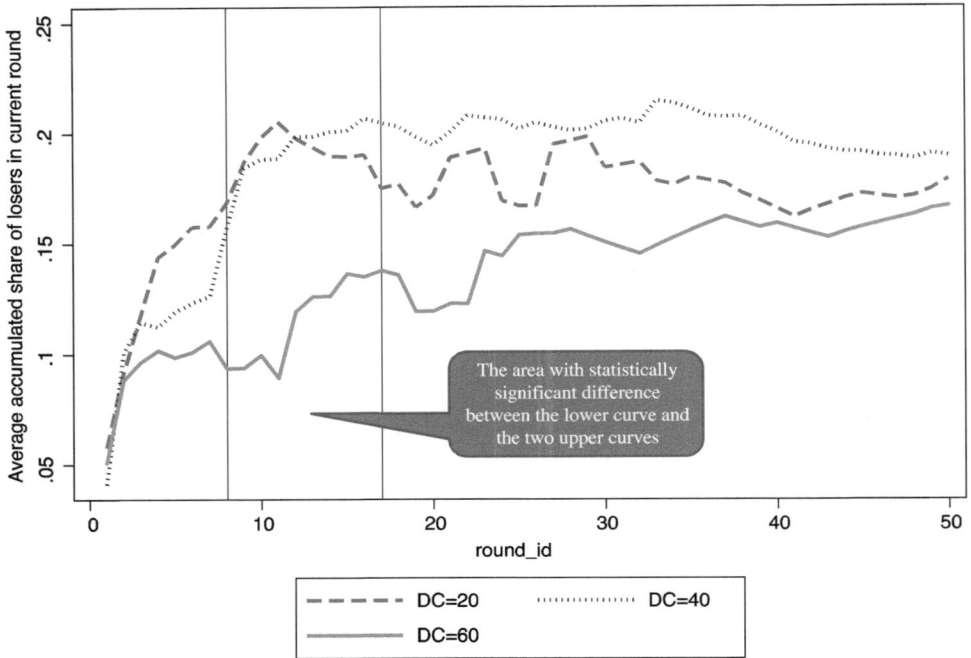

Fig. 6. Current losers' average accumulated shares by defection costs

3. The surprising part, however, is the fact that they caught up at all. They did not turn the table by reaching the one-third line and become winners, but they were far from having nothing as one would expect under a tyranny of the majority. Just looking at the initial losers may not give us the whole picture. The fact that initial losers were not terribly worse off at the end does not necessarily imply that there is no tyranny of the majority because other original winners may have become the victims instead. This is why I am also offering figure 6 to show the accumulated share of the players who received the least amount in their tables until a given round, regardless of who the initial losers were. In other words, a data point of (10, 0.1) would imply that at the round 10 the average losing player has received 0.1 of the total benefit from his table so far.

Figure 6 differs from figure 5 in the way the tails of the curves are much lower. This means that, although the initial losers tend to catch up, new losers will emerge and distributive outcomes are not completely equal. However, it is important not to overinterpret the bad luck of the winners-turned-losers because they could use the same uncertainty built into the system to cycle back into the winning coalition. As long as winners alternate, players that adopt the same strategies should approach the same relative outcome in the very long run because of the Law of Large Numbers, just as in a fair-dice gambling game.

Comparing the three curves in figure 6, we can tell that there is no significant difference between the top two curves. Their average gap widened in the later rounds, but the number of tables that were still playing also decreased, so the statistical difference remains insignificant. This is hardly surprising considering the players' failure to adopt anticycling strategies. In fact, the chance of winning coalition change in the medium-defection-cost tables is even slightly higher than in the low-defection-cost tables (30.3 vs. 26.2 percent), although a *t*-test does not show statistical significance.

When comparing the high-defection-cost category to each of the other two categories, differences in distributive outcomes can be observed. Such differences may not seem impressive at a first glance because they last for only a few rounds, but they are informative nonetheless.

First, it certainly takes time for the effect to show. In the first two rounds, almost every table has a highly unequal distribution, exactly because cycling has yet to start. As previously mentioned, individual proposals tend to be highly unequal, with a very small, if any, share offered to the losing player. Therefore, before the losing players figure out how to induce defection by the winning ones, the accumulated share will stay unequal. However, the differences start to show at round 3 and become statistically significant after a few more rounds. The high-defection-cost category remains highly unequal while the other categories start to improve their equality. Such difference exactly results from the fact that defections are more common in medium- and low-defection-cost tables. The chance that defection will happen under high defection costs is significantly lower than that number under low or medium defection costs (verified by a *t*-test). Taking the reciprocals of the probabilities of defection can give us the expected duration of winning coalitions. A winning coalition is expected to last 3.3 and 3.8 rounds, respectively, under low and medium defection costs and 6.5 rounds under high defection costs.

What is even more interesting, however, is the fact that the statistical difference between high-defection-cost group and the other groups starts to disappear as the game goes on. Surprisingly, even with a lower frequency, defections still happened once in a while in high-defection-cost tables, which eventually helped the losers to catch up. Of course, unlike the low- and median-defection-cost groups, the initial losers in these tables normally were unable to beat the initial winners in terms of accumulated benefits, but this overall long-run inequality is not much worse.

I offer three possible explanations for why it happens. First, a virtual negotiation table is, after all, different from a real-world legislature in the way in which losers can easily exit. Other than the moderate prize offered by the experimenter, there is no mechanism that can prevent a losing player from quitting the table. Exit therefore becomes a tool of deterrence for the tyranny of the majority. When winners are enjoying the game, they may be concerned with the sudden disruption of the game that is caused by another player's exit. So one of them may defect to the loser just to keep him at the table. This threat of quitting the game is probably the reason why even some of the worst dictators will leave a mouthful of food to their subjects. Second, one player wrote to me after the game to state that she had offered to form a coalition with a losing player simply out of sympathy. This is certainly a factor that affects any rational-choice experimental study (Rabin 1993) even though my design of the online negotiation already reduced players' moral concerns to a large extent. Finally, players can make mistakes. They can simply forget who the coalition partner in the last round was or even ignore the existence of defection costs. These are all small-probability events, but they can accumulate enough to reduce the long-run stability of the coalitions.

In general, we can see the following patterns revealed by the experiment.

1. In the short run, each individual proposal passed is likely to be highly unequal, benefiting a majority at the expense of a minority, consistent with the dominant beliefs in the literature of short-run divide-a-dollar games. This also results in very low accumulated shares for losers in all groups in the first few rounds.
2. As the game continues, the shares of the losers in tables with low and medium defection costs quickly improve while those in tables with high defection costs remain poor for a longer period. That difference is statistically significant only from rounds 8 to 17, but it is visible throughout the game.
3. In the long run, all groups maintain a moderate level of inequality of accumulated wealth, although the initial winners and losers are more likely to switch positions in low- and medium-defection-cost groups.

Connecting the Experiment to Real Politics

One could certainly doubt whether the variation in equality between different game tables can really imply that between polities with different institutions. I now address the threats to the external validity of the experiment one at a time. Some of them, as I will show, are rather legitimate concerns. However, if the experiment results agree with observational data from cross-national comparisons, which I present in the next chapter, these threats should not significantly undermine our confidence in the external validity of the experiment.

(1) Number of Players

One of the most intuitive differences between the experiment and the negotiations in a real voting body is the number of players. Not only do many legislatures have more than three parties, but each party is not always a unitary actor. This issue was addressed in the previous chapter where I laid out the theory for the three-player game. I briefly repeat them there. First, excluding the players that are too small to affect the outcome, the number of pivotal parties is very often three or less. Second, when there is a unified majority party, the number of players within minorities is not consequential. Third, the case in which there are more than three significant parties should behave in a cyclical way and therefore cannot be distinguished from the low-defection-cost scenario with three players. Fourth, when there are only two significant players, they are equivalent to three players with high defection costs. See the last chapter for more detailed arguments.

(2) The Time Dimension

Because statistical significance only lasts a few rounds in each game, it is reasonable to doubt whether these rounds really represent a significant time period in the real world. In other words, how long is one round in the real world? If each round takes only a week, does it mean that high defection costs will delay minority interests for a few months?

There are several alternatives for interpreting the negotiation cycle in the game. We can consider one round to be one legislative decision, one major budget bill, or one electoral cycle. Unfortunately, there is no convincing reason to prefer one alternative to another. However, I argue that in any cycle a duration of ten rounds is not an insignificant period.

When assuming each legislative decision to be one round of negotiation, we should exclude bills without significant distributive effects, which could include programmatic policies, procedural legislation, and minor regulations such as traffic rules. Legislative decisions that are truly consequential to a minority, such as taxation, welfare, and religious and cultural policies, do not happen on a weekly basis. Even if they do happen frequently, we cannot expect the opposition parties to induce defections at such a fast pace. In parliamentary systems where legislative coalitions are indistinguishable from governing coalitions, opposition legislative successes have to be exceptions instead of common events in any given cabinet cycle. In presidential or semipresidential systems, opposition legislative success is also hard to achieve, though in a different way. Because the governing coalition (which is really a single person) is different from the legislative coalition in these countries, legislative coalitions can be more flexible. However, considering that most executive presidents have either veto power or exclusive agenda-setting power (Shugart 1999: 68), any legislation that opposes the presidential preference is hard to pass, if at all, without first removing the incumbent president. Even in a country where the president has little legislative power, the fact that he controls the executive means that he can choose to expend less effort to implement a bill he dislikes. For these reasons, the number of opportunities for oppositions' legislative success in any given administration under any political system must be small, and therefore it is not helpful to count each short time period between two legislative decisions as one round.

As a result, two conditions need to be met in order for defections to make a difference in the game. First, the time duration between two rounds of the game has to be long enough for a minority to find an opportunity to strike. Second, each round of the game has to be consequential enough to be worth the cost of cycling. In other words, a defection has to be for a major distributive negotiation in order to be worth its cost.

How should we decide which types of distributive negotiations are "major"? There are two likely candidates. The first way is to assume each annual fiscal budget to be one round because that budget determines the distribution of the largest faction of state resources and is worth fighting for by each party and interest group. It means that the duration of each round in the experiment should be thought of as a calendar year. Since the average coalition duration in the experiment is 3.8 rounds under low defection costs and 6.5 rounds under high defection costs, such an assumption means that we should expect the winning coalition of the annual budget to last 2.7 years longer when defection costs are high. Note that such a difference is very similar to the life expectancy differences found in the next chapter using the executive power alternation dataset.

It also implies that a loser's accumulated share of the annual budget will be significantly higher under low defection costs than under high defection costs during the time period between the fifth and fifteenth calendar years. If Svolic (2008) is right that the first 20 years are the crucial period for determining whether a democracy can consolidate, that difference will matter not for minorities per se but for the survival of the whole system.

Another way to interpret the experiment is to assume each round to be equivalent to one electoral cycle. That way we should expect countries with low defection costs to have a power alternation every four election cycles, assuming there are no external shocks such as scandals or recessions, while those with high defection costs will have a power alternation every six election cycles. In that case, the difference between high- and low-defection-cost institutions in terms of losers' share will last from the fifth to the fifteenth electoral cycles, a period long enough to justify lowering defection costs for the sake of minority protection. Such an interpretation also means that the first alternation is expected to come two elections earlier in low-defection-cost scenarios.

(3) Level of Defection Costs

Do the defection cost levels in the experimental setting (20, 40, and 60 percent) truly reflect those in different institutional settings? Even if 50 percent is a theoretically meaningful cutoff point between high and low defection costs, does it really demarcate a coalition government as opposed to a majority or presidential government? This is a tough question to answer because (1) it is hard to measure defection costs in the field and (2) there are large variations within each institutional category because of unobserved factors.

However, I argue that the actual cutoff point may not be important as long as we know that one institutional alternative implies higher defection costs than the other. Under a coalition government, at least we know that the defection costs in either budget negotiation or government formation is more likely to be low for defecting politicians, even though there is a chance that they will be pushed above the 50 percent threshold by other institutional or non-institutional factors. Under a presidential or one-party parliamentary government, the opposite is true.

In general, none of these threats to the external validity of the experiment can be completely dismissed. However, there are still strong reasons, as elaborated in this section, for us to believe that distributive patterns and the strategic mechanism they reveal are generally applicable regardless of the number of players, the time duration, and the level of treatment. Experimental studies in social science tend to be unrealistic because societies by definition are hard to simulate. But because of their strong internal validity, achieved through randomization, they are very useful in verifying and explaining certain patterns that are observed using real-world data.

Conclusion

In response to the difficulties of operationalizing the electoral losers' bargaining power under majority rule, I conducted a novel experimental study inspired by online board games. The players are separated into small virtual negotiation tables to distribute their prizes repeatedly under majority rule. Different tables are randomly assigned different levels of penalty for those who defect from the winning coalition. It turns out that it takes much longer for tables with high defection costs to achieve a winning coalition change. As a result, it also takes much longer for the original losers in these groups to accumulate wealth through inducing defections.

The external validity of such an approach is no doubt vulnerable. This is why I review the evidence from a series of cross-national studies in the next chapter. These observed patterns of different institutional arrangements may not be able to serve as direct tests of the defection cost effect because of the existence of many other explanations and confounding variables. But when viewed together with the experiment results, they make such a theory more cognitively appealing.

FIVE

Exploring the Defection Cost Argument with Observational Data

In the last two chapters, I analyzed the simplest possible scenario of distributive policy making in a democratic context, a three-player divide-a-dollar game. I show that in systems with higher defection costs, electoral losers have a harder time catching up because of the difficulty of breaking up the winning coalitions. The experiment result is not as clear-cut as the model suggests, but it does show some significant differences between types of groups, at least in the early stage of the game. However, does this simple game tell us anything about how actual democracies distribute their resources? How much do the restrictive assumptions in the model and the experiment threaten the external validity of the result? In this chapter, I discuss in detail some observational data from the existing literature and explain how they are largely consistent with the three-player model predictions.

What Real World Institutions Are Associated with Defection Costs?

An obvious difficulty with such a test is that no political system can quantitatively stipulate how much a player has to pay to exit a coalition. However, based on the existing literature, there exist some institutional variables that have clear implications for defection costs and therefore can serve as proxies.

First, let us consider the costs incurred by legislators in a winning coalition who vote against the majority preference. Numerous contextual reasons, such as ideological distance and specific constituency interests, can affect legislators' defection decisions. These reasons vary from bill to bill and are not directly related to a country's institutional choice. The key variable I focus on is whether the winning coalition members belong to the same party organization and share the same party label. When a single majority party exists, defection from that party implies voting against one's more important political label and signals disagreement among politicians who are described by a common policy bundle and ideological characteristic. The most immediate cost of doing that would be making a politician subject to disciplinary penalties imposed by his party organization, which could include withdrawal of a nomination (Whiteley and Seyd 1999: 55), reduced chance of a cabinet promotion (Benedetto and Hix 2007), or a drop in rank on the party list. Even if the party decides to forgo punishment, acting against one's party will surely decrease the candidate's ability to communicate with voters. Since party membership is the most convenient way for voters to evaluate a candidate (Popkin 1994), candidates that are less partisan may have a harder time explaining which ideologies or voter groups they represent.

Of course, even in a country where the winning coalition is composed of different parties, defection is not without cost. An unreliable coalition partner may have trouble finding partners in the future (Tavits 2008). However, that cost of interparty defection is not nearly as formidable as that of intraparty defection simply because the former does not involve a conflict with one's most significant political label. Such difference easily can be seen in the legislative voting pattern presented by Cheibub et al. (2004: 578). They show that the legislative success of the chief executive is much more common when there exists a majority party, a pattern that is true in both presidential and parliamentary systems.

The costs incurred by governing party/coalition legislators who realign themselves with oppositions within the legislature does not capture the whole picture of the defection cost variation. Keep in mind that there are also groups in the society that are not represented in the legislature. Some groups are unrepresented because they do not participate in the voting process. But, since this book is mainly concerned with the majority-minority relationship under majority rule, let us only focus on those who vote but fail to gain representation. Such groups are certainly common in disproportional systems, especially single-seat-district systems. They cannot rely on legislative bargaining to split the winning coalition because they have no legislative power with which to bargain. Some groups may be represented but have much smaller seat shares compared to their national vote shares due to disproportionality. They may be able to induce defection from the winning coalition, but the concession they offer would have to be large because of the small number of seats they could use as leverage.

For unrepresented and underrepresented groups, legislative realignment is not a very useful tool. But they can resort to another type of realignment, which is realignment at the electoral level. Instead of persuading legislators from other parties to vote for their interests, they could persuade voters who usually vote for other parties to jump ship and convert to their own parties. In order to do that, they certainly have to offer concessions by adjusting their parties' policy platforms. For example, if an underrepresented ethnic group wants to gain more seats for its party, it could add gay rights to its original platform as a way to attract gay rights supporters from other ethnic groups. The group members might not be supportive of gay rights per se, but it might be useful to make such concessions because their party needs a larger voter base to defy the Duvergerian disadvantages in a disproportional system and gain bargaining power in the legislature. So, as long as a country's electoral process is intact, political losers can hope for some realignment given smart strategies and good luck.

However, realignment at the electoral level differs greatly from realignment at the legislative level in that the former is much more costly. Instead of negotiating with a number of legislators, those who hope to split the winning coalition will have to convey their messages to an ocean of voters and acquire their feedback in return. It is impossible to accurately estimate how many voters will change their minds giving certain concessions. The cost is further exacerbated by the fact that elections only occur every few years. An underrepresented minority does not have the freedom to choose the optimal time to initiate cycling because the timing of the election is either predetermined or, in case of parliamentary systems, a result of governing parties' strategic maneuvering (Lupia and Strøm 1995).

The difficulty of realignment caused by unrepresented voters is most obvious in presidential and semipresidential systems. Any presidential election by definition will leave a large number of voters without representation in the executive branch (Linz 1990a; Lijphart 1999). This is simply because a presidency, unlike a legislature, is not a combination of a governing side and an opposing side but an indivisible entity. In order for the unrepresented groups to "cycle" into the winning coalition, a large number of voters, not just legislators, will have to switch allegiance, which will not have a chance to materialize until another election is due.

It is true that cycling can still happen between elections in the legislative branch of a presidential or semipresidential system. In fact, presidents are less likely than prime ministers to have legislative success, as Cheibub et al. (2004: 578) show, because their interests are less closely aligned with those of legislature. But this does not mean that opposition groups are more powerful in presidential systems. They may be more likely to successfully block legislation due to the greater number of veto players, but there are two more important roles that they have virtually no power to play. First, when a president has veto power, it implies that any status quo change in legislation that goes against the presidential preference is nearly impossible. In contrast, in a multiparty parliamentary system, new legislation that goes against the prime minister's preference is also rare, but it does happen occasionally as long as the opposition parties manage to find ad hoc defectors from the winning coalition. For example, in June 2017, Germany passed the gay marriage law even though Chancellor Merkel voted against it. Second, and more important, opposition legislators in presidential systems have very limited influence on which laws will be enforced. This is because, unlike those in parliamentary systems, they do not have an institutional tool with which to threaten the job security of the chief executive. Even a massive defection among legislators from the presidential party does not pose an immediate threat to the president personally or the branch that is accountable to him. A more explicit example is President Obama's use of Deferred Action for Childhood Arrival as a means of defying immigration legislation. But in most cases, such executive policy changes happen in a low-profile way in closed-door cabinet meetings without even being noticed. The Trump administration's controversial zero-tolerance immigration policy, which included separation of child immigrants from their parents, was not intended to be highly publicized and became known only after a series of investigative reports. The two presidents' opposite policies on immigration enforcement both happened without the endorsement of the legislative branch. Presidents' enormous power over law enforcement agencies, ensured by their ability to appoint and dismiss executive officials, means that opposition parties, as well as the voters they represent, tend to stay on the losing side of the policy until the next election.

Another phenomenon that is related to the defection cost in presidential systems is the presidentialization of parties (a concept elaborated in Samuels and Shugart 2010). Even though legislators in a presidential or semipresidential system have their separate constituencies, their job security can still be affected by their alignment with their parties' presidents or presidential candidates. Recent developments in American politics have made this phenomenon extremely visible. The US Congress was famous for its lack of party discipline throughout most of its history, which resulted in high rates of cross-voting (see Jacobson 2013: 261–65). A few decades ago we could argue that the United States is a low-defection-cost system with occasional legislative successes by opposition parties. But that has gradually changed over time (265–66). In the Trump era, congressional politics has reached a point where it is unimaginable for most Republican lawmakers to defy the president or for most Democratic ones to engage in the slightest cooperation with him. Such a level of polarization seems to have become an equilibrium with no turning back.

Of course, the US legislative outcome is complicated by the existence of midterm elections. The extremely short election cycle of House members means that an opposition party has more chances of disturbing the winning coalition at the electoral level, which may partially counter an overly powerful president in the second half of his term. But in general we can safely argue that the winning coalition is more stable in the United States than in countries where the survival of the executive branch depends on multiple parties and winning coalition realignment can happen without a new election.

Based on this analysis, we can tell that the cost of winning coalition realignment is high when there exists either a majority party or an executive presidency, which implies that realignment of the winning coalition normally can only happen at the electoral level. Electoral losers in these cases cannot seek an alternative winning coalition until the next scheduled election, which involves high information costs of communicating directly with a large number of voters. Therefore, if the observational data reveal that the no-majority and weak-presidency scenario, namely, coalition or minority government, is indeed more friendly to electoral losers, this may serve to support the model prediction and experiment results discussed in previous chapters. Of course, even if such a relationship exists, one can offer explanations other than the defection cost mechanism. However, as I demonstrate shortly, since many different proxies of defection costs and distributive equality all point to the same positive relationship, and since the experiment result is consistent with that relationship, the underlying theory is hard to reject. In each of the following sections, I introduce one branch of empirical studies that addresses the issue and mention why existing theories are insufficient in explaining these patterns.

The Effects of Institutions on General Equality
and the Size of Redistribution

In chapter 3, I discussed the problems of using general equality and redistribution to measure minority protection. The normative implications of such measures are highly dependent on a person's ideological placement on the left-right dimension. However, these works are still worth discussing since their dependent variables still weakly proxy different systems' attitudes toward disadvantaged minorities. Greater income equality in a society normally implies that less of the population is left out of the overall prosperity.

It is arguable that such equality can be overdone to the extent of hurting its objectives (Friedman 1962: 179), but at least equality implies that few segments of a society are treated tyrannically. It is also arguable that less equal societies can have rather benign governments since inequality can result from laissez-faire competition (Smith 1977 [1776] 593). However, at least we cannot exclude the possibility that the government is adopting certain redistributive measures in order to hurt minorities. In other words, governments in unequal societies are not necessarily tyrannical, but they are more suspicious.

Lijphart's (1969, 1977, 1999) series of studies is most influential in this tradition. In testing the institutional effects of the rich-poor ratio variable from the United Nations Development Program, he finds that the equality difference between majoritarian and consensus democracies on the executive-parties dimension is significant before or after controlling development level and with or without extreme cases (Lijphart 1999: 283). The same is true when testing other variables that Lijphart deems as measuring the "kindness and gentleness" of a democracy.

Although Lijphart has defined his "consensus democracy on the executive-parties dimension" concept using a large set of variables, some of which have little to do with defection costs, it is not unrelated to my defection costs argument. This is because the cases that are considered consensual democracies by his standard almost all happen to be parliamentary systems without a unified majority party,[1] while the cases that are included in majoritarian democracies all happen to be countries that either tend to have a strong majority party or have a non-figurehead presidency. Therefore, such a typology happens to be consistent with the defection

---

1. Japan is the only country in these cases that tends to have a majority party during LDP (Liberal Democratic Party) dominance, but the highly independent LDP factions and frequent changes of leadership should also qualify it as a low-defection-cost system.

costs typology introduced in chapter 3. At least based on Lijphart's sample, countries with lower defection costs tend to have more equal wealth distributions.

Although they approach it from a different angle, Persson and Tabellini (2003: 163) essentially confirm the same finding. The dependent variables they use are various measures of the size of government. Such a measure, of course, is even more normatively controversial than economic equality because its connection with equality is purely based on progressive redistribution, which I have shown lacks clear normative consensus. But if we add a stronger normative assumption, which Lijphart (1999) implies, that minorities should be taken care of by the welfare state, then the size of government may actually imply a better government attitude toward minorities.

What Persson and Tabellini (2003: 163) find is that both proportionality and parliamentarism have a significant effect on increasing government size. This, again, can certainly be used to argue against the said systems on efficiency grounds, but at least it shows that countries with low defection costs seem to have done more for disadvantaged groups.

Similarly, Iversen and Soskice's (2006: 165) cross-national study shows that "center-left governments dominate under PR [proportional representation] systems, whereas center-right governments dominate under majoritarian systems." Like those in Lijphart (1999) and Persson and Tabellini (2003), the patterns found in this piece cannot help us make clear normative choices without a certain ideological premise. Both their deductive model and empirical data are restricted to mature democracies that conform to the progressive distribution assumption (Iversen and Soskice 2006: 167) and therefore cannot help us determine which systems are more likely to engage in discriminative policies. However, their finding at least implies a more pro-equality and pro-minority characteristic of proportional systems, which serves as another verification of the same pattern as the other pieces.

In sum, there is little controversy in the literature over whether low-defection-cost types of political institutions are empirically associated with greater equality. Whether such equality is normatively favorable may be subject to debate because the dependent variables in these studies do not distinguish laissez-faire inequality from state-imposed inequality.

The Effect of Institutions on Intrastate Conflict

The frequency and intensity of intrastate conflict may serve as another proxy of minority protection. According to the classical arguments on divided societies, one of the key factors that make a country vulnerable to conflict is that "only demographic change, drastic electoral revision, coup d'état, or all-out ethnic warfare can convert opposition into the government" (Horowitz 1985: 348–49). If a society is free of conflict, this more or less implies that there is an easier mechanism through which to please the electoral losers.

However, the cross-national tests using conflict variables may not be very informative because large-scale violence is after all a low-probability event in any democratic system, let alone established democracies. If our purpose is to compare subcategories of democratic institutions, conflict variables are unlikely to have enough cross-country variations, especially between countries with similar developmental levels. For example, in the widely cited research of Fearon and Laitin (2003) on ethnic conflict and insurgency, only 14 of 111 cases of conflict happened under a freely elected government that had been in place for at least one year. With such a small number of notable conflicts, making comparisons between democratic subcategories is not statistically meaningful.

However, even with only 14 cases (see table 5 for a complete list), I find at least some visible, though not robust, patterns that may support the defection cost theory. First, the 1974 conflict in Cyprus listed in the table should be excluded from consideration because it was really an international proxy war between Greece, which staged a coup in Cyprus, and Turkey, which in turn invaded the country (Adamson 2001). That left me with 13 cases of truly intrastate conflict under freely elected governments. And the patterns found in these cases are interesting. Five of these cases happened under presidential or semipresidential systems in which the president directly commanded the executive through his dismissal power.[2] In the remaining eight cases, seven happened under one-party majority governments. Both of these institutions are considered to have high defection costs according to my earlier typology. This means that there is only one case in Fearon and Laitin's (2003) dataset in which an intrastate conflict, the 1977 conflict in Turkey, happened under a fragmented parliamentary system.

Although they are intuitively striking, these observations are certainly insufficient to make a clear-cut argument. Besides the small sample size, one should be especially cautious about the endogeneity of democratic scores to conflict. Since democracy is measured by Polity scores (Marshall,

---

2. This is known as a president-parliamentary system according to Shugart and Carey's (1992) definition.

Jaggers, and Gurr 2014), the reason some cases are excluded may not be their lack of democratic institutions but their inability to hold free and fair elections under ethnic tension. It is hard to predict whether the inclusion of these cases would undermine the institutional prediction. Nonetheless, if Fearon and Laitin's (2003) data tell us anything about the effects of democracies' subcategories, it offers another weak confirmation of my defection costs argument. A more robust finding that supports my argument can be found in Wilkinson (2004). Recognizing the various difficulties involved in conducting cross-national studies on ethnic conflict between democratic countries (9–10), he focuses on comparing different states within India, a highly rich pool for intracountry variation. It is true that the electoral systems and executive types are the same across Indian states, but Wilkinson's key independent variable also has obvious implications for defection costs.

The central finding of Wilkinson is that the Indian states with more fragmented party systems, as measured by the effective number of vote-winning parties, tend to have less ethnic conflict between Hindus and Muslims. His explanation is that if a state has salient intra-Hindu cleavages, such as those between caste-based parties, Hindu politicians may have to rely on Muslim votes to win offices. Therefore they have stronger incentives to order law enforcement to prevent ethnic riots.

Although Wilkinson does not use the same term, his theory is similar in spirit to the defection costs argument I make because his key explanatory variable, party fragmentation in the electorate, essentially proxies the like-

TABLE 5. Ethnic Conflict and Insurgency Cases under Elected Governments

Country	Year	Polity Score	Presidential or President-Premier Systems	One-Party Majority Government
Costa Rica	1948	10	Yes	
Colombia	1963	7	Yes	
Peru	1981	7	Yes	
UK (Northern Ireland)	1969	10	No	Yes
~~Cyprus~~[a]	~~1974~~	~~10~~	~~No~~	~~No~~
Central African Republic	1996	6	Yes	
Turkey	1977	9	No	No
Turkey	1984	7	No	Yes
India	1982	8	No	Yes
India	1989	8	No	Yes
Pakistan	1993	8	No	Yes
Burma	1948	8	No	Yes
Sri Lanka	1971	8	No	Yes
Sri Lanka	1983	5	Yes	

[a]This case is essentially an interstate war, and therefore should be disregarded from consideration here.

lihood of winner alternation through voter realignment. His key micro-mechanism, intervention by state armed forces, is not a typical distributive policy per se. But, as I discussed extensively in chapter 2, such intervention is still distributive in a broad sense, essentially trading the psychological excitement of the religious fundamentalists for the physical security of the moderate believers.

Of course, Wilkinson's book is one step short of extending his conclusion to the choice of electoral systems because of the lack of institutional variation among Indian states. But such a choice is very much implied. If fragmented party systems are conducive to ethnic peace, so are permissive electoral systems if we believe proportionality can help any majority group express its intragroup cleavages. Whether proportional systems would work under a unidimensional cleavage structure is certainly a source of contention in the literature, as I reviewed in detail in chapter 1, but let us leave that question to chapters 6 and 7.

The Effects of Institutions on Performance and Stability

One of the first panel data analyses of subcategories of democracies is by Cheibub et al. (1996). Their key dependent variable is the durability of democracy, which is certainly not a direct measure of distributive outcomes. However, democratic breakdown, just like ethnic conflict, in a way approximates the difficulties electoral losers face in keeping a share within the existing institutional framework.

Again, a parliamentary-proportional combination stands out in the data of Cheibub et al. (1996: 45–46) as the most durable type of democracy. According to their calculation, "Democracy's life expectancy under presidentialism is less than 20 years, while under parliamentarism it is 71 years" and "The difference in durability is not an effect of the levels of economic development." Among all the parliamentary systems, "those in which one party had a majority of seats in the lower house of the legislature have an expected life of 55 years, while parliamentary systems without a one-party majority have an expected life of 111 years."

Like the other studies reviewed earlier, this piece certainly cannot directly verify my argument. In fact the authors cite many other theories in order to explain the durability of proportional parliamentary systems (Linz 1990a, 1990b; Mainwaring and Shugart 1994). However, better minority protection can at least serve as one of the potential explanations.

Gerring and Thacker (2008) provide another important study on performance variations among subcategories of democracies. They did not focus on any single dependent variable but rather employed a long list of performance proxies ranging from telephone mainlines to infant mortality. They find support for their main institutional combinations: unitarism, parliamentarism, and closed-list PR. Even though their overall institutional recommendation is different from that made in this book, it does include the same two components: parliamentarism and proportionality.

It is true that the theory Gerring and Thacker (2008) use to explain these institutions' better performance is completely different from mine. However, I argue that their theory is less convincing than their empirics. The mechanism they use to justify the three-element institutional combination is that they all promote a centripetal tendency in the policy-making process. The authors prefer parliamentarism, unitarism and closed-list PR because they all promote unified ideological parties and discourage locally oriented policies. However, it is questionable whether these institutions are truly centripetal and, in case they are, whether centripetalism truly explains their better performance.

First, among parliamentary systems it is hard to argue that closed-list PR is necessarily more centripetal than other electoral systems. The Westminster system in the United Kingdom, despite its locally elected legislators, is famous for its "efficient secret" (Cox 1987), a highly party-oriented and nonclientelistic policy style. Legislators are loyal to their parties regardless of their different origins (146). Aware of these characteristics in their own parliament, voters elect local representatives as their agents in choosing national leaders and therefore focus more on their ideological affiliation than their local policy positions (136).

Similarly, it is also questionable whether presidential systems are less centripetal than parliamentarism if the president is powerful enough to overrule the legislature. Is a single elected policy maker not more centripetal than a large body with hundreds of policy makers? Gerring and Thacker argue that disagreement between branches of the government makes a presidential system less centripetal and more subject to a series of legislative and bureaucratic deficiencies (2008: 69–80), but that will only be true under the assumption that the legislature has the capacity to restrain the presidency, which is not true in a large part of the developing world.

Second, even if these institutional features have a centripetal tendency, it is questionable whether such a tendency is sufficient to explain good performance. In fact, there could be many other ways to make a political system even more centripetal than what the Gerring and Thacker propose, such as eliminating local autonomy completely by replacing locally elected

governors and mayors with central government appointees or removing
local legislative demands by installing unlimited presidential decree power.
In other words, the most centripetal system one can imagine is an elected
dictatorship, such as the unlimited Russian presidency, in which the president alone wields decree power assisted by veto power to prevent over-
rides (Shugart 1999: 64). Gerring and Thacker's logic cannot tell us why
centripetalism has to stop at a certain level and why legislatures and locally
accountable governments are necessary at all. For these reasons, Gerring
and Thacker's empirical results may be less supportive of their own theory
than of the defection cost explanation.

The Effect of Institutions on Power Alternation

Another way of testing defection cost effects is to compare different systems' frequency of power alternation. Although this variable does not
directly measure minorities' interests, it implies electoral losers' bargaining
power and the likelihood of entering the winning coalition. To my knowledge, there are no existing studies that directly target this variable. Therefore, I provide a brief analysis in this section, using a change of the chief
executive's party membership as a measure of power alternation.

It should be cautioned that the party alternation of a chief executive
is not entirely equivalent to the winning coalition change modeled in the
previous chapter. Sometimes, even though the party composition of a
coalition changes significantly, the prime minister can be controlled by the
same party (such as control of the Italian prime ministerial position by the
Christian Democratic Party from 1946 to 1981 under different coalitions).
Theoretically, it is also possible that a change in the partisanship of a chief
executive may simply be a result of the changing balance within a coalition
and therefore does not imply a new coalition. However, regardless of these
subtle differences, it is hard to deny that partisanship change of the chief
executive, the single most important office (or offices given dual-executive
systems), is a strong indicator that the winners and losers in a polity have
experienced a significant degree of realignment. If we can tell under which
systems such realignment is more frequent, we may be able to explain the
differences in distributive policies.

The most complete data on partisanship of chief executives is from
Samuels and Shugart (2010). Merging these data with those of Bormann
and Golder (2013) and Li and Shugart (2016) results in a dataset that cov-

ers a large number of the chief executives elected between 1946 and 2007 with both institutional variables and partisan variables. I first calculate the length of each democratic period in each country from the dataset and then count the number of power alternations that happened during that period. Dividing the former by the latter can easily give us the life expectancy of governing parties in each institutional category.

I have found that the life expectancy of an average presidential party is 8.5 years. When excluding semipresidential systems, in which presidents are not necessarily chief executives (Shugart 2005), that number is 6.6 years. In contrast, the life expectancy of an average prime ministerial party is just 4.7 years. Excluding semipresidential systems will raise that number to 5.2. Whether including semipresidential systems or not, the same pattern holds: presidential parties are more durable than prime ministerial parties. However, as I show next, such differences may not have resulted from the executive types per se but for more subtle reasons.

In the next step, I divide parliamentary systems into two subgroups, those with a proportional tier (including list PR, single-transferable-vote, and multitier systems) and those without such a tier (all other systems). I found that the life expectancy of prime ministerial parties in the former group is just 4.6 years while that of the latter is 6.0 years. Since the latter group of electoral systems is much more likely to produce a single majority party, such a result suggests that majoritarian party systems are more likely to have durable governing parties.

In order to further verify these results, I divide parliamentary systems using another criterion: whether there exists a majority party in the parliament. The difference turns out to be even stronger. The life expectancy of a prime ministerial party with more than 50 percent of the seats is as long as 8.1 years while that of a prime ministerial party with 50 percent or fewer seats is only 4.1 years.

It is hard to say which of these typologies is more helpful. Dividing parliamentary systems by electoral systems has the benefit of freedom from endogeneity because electoral systems can be considered exogenous to power alternation. But dividing them by the existence of majority parties has the benefit of better capturing the more immediate neighbor in the causal chain. The defection costs, after all, are not directly explained by proportionality but by whether the majority shares the same party label. However, I do not intend to discuss this tradeoff further because the two tests point to the same conclusion: majoritarian party systems (or the institutions that promote such systems) result in longer life expectancy of the governing party. Table 6 summarizes the results in all pure presidential and parliamentary systems. These results show that even though presidential parties seem to be more durable than prime-ministerial parties in general, they are no more durable, if not less so, than those under majoritarian electoral systems. The difference between executive types almost entirely comes from those prime ministers that need more than one party's confidence to stay in office.

Party alternation can certainly be explained by the events that affect voters' perception of the incumbent's valence scores, such as recessions or scandals. But if we assume that different systems have a similar probability of having such valence-related shocks, the difference in governing parties' life expectancy has to be explained by the cycling of winning coalitions. What these patterns tell us, therefore, is that parliamentary systems with coalition governments are much more likely to see party alternation of chief executives than other systems are.

What is shown here may not be surprising. But exactly because of its intuitiveness, no one bothers to calculate the actual differences. It is important to officially confirm such a pattern since it establishes the connection between institutions and a crucial intermediate variable: how fast political power changes hands.

Just testing power alternation is certainly not enough since the causal relationship between alternation and policy outcomes is still unclear. But such a test does provide us with an important insight into institutional choice. Even though we still lack a deductive theory in the literature to link such alternation to any normatively favorable dependent variables, it is a common premise in the discipline to consider power alternation as an important sign of the health of democracy. In their datasets, for example, Pzreworski et al. (2000) and Bormann and Golder (2013) all code a country democratic only if it has experienced power alternation of the chief executive.

TABLE 6. Life Expectancy of a Chief Executive's Party (years)

	All	Without Proportional Tier	With Proportional Tier	With Majority Party	Without Majority Party
Presidential systems	6.6	N/A	N/A	N/A	N/A
Parliamentary systems	5.2	6.0	4.6	8.1	4.1

Conclusion

In this chapter, I reviewed a large number of famous large-N comparative studies that test many different variables regarding policy outcomes and performances. Regardless of their extremely diverse theoretical focuses, they interestingly imply almost the same normative preferences of political institutions, which is a coalition government under a parliamentary system. Such a normative preference is consistent with the defection costs argument I made in the last two chapters.

Both the experimental approach in the last chapter and cross-national studies reviewed in this one are far from perfect. The former suffers from the lack of external validity that results from the simplistic setting of the game while the latter has to employ proxy variables that do not perfectly measure distributive inequality or defection costs. However, the fact that they point in the same direction can offer us cognitive confidence that the underlying theory makes sense. Having a fragmented winning coalition that is subject to defection may be the key to explaining why some democracies treat their minorities better than others, as well as why democracies in general behave much better than alternative systems do in that regard.

SIX

Is There Such a Thing as a Majority Group?

A Theory of Majority Splitting under Proportional Systems

With the help of an online experiment and verification from the existing empirical data, I reached a conclusion that potential defection from the winning coalition is a key factor that keeps a democracy from falling into a tyranny of the majority. Even though not every party can enter the cabinet or the winning side of a legislative vote, the losers in the game can always cycle into the winning coalition, making sure that the long-term distributive outcomes are relatively equal.

However, from an institutional design perspective, what is the point of knowing such a phenomenon? Is it possible to artificially design the defection cost of a winning coalition? We know that certain electoral systems are associated with multiparty coalitions, which are easier to break than a single-party majority, but how strong is the causal relationship? Could a unidimensional cleavage make a fragmented majority impossible? The literature has not reached a consensus. This and the next chapter are devoted to these questions.

The Puzzle: Can Majority Parties Survive Proportionality?

From an institutional design perspective, it is not enough to know that the lack of a stable majority party is favorable in divided societies. We still need to determine whether there are institutional solutions that can make it harder for such a party to persist. It is certainly a bad idea to artificially stipulate that there be no majority parties. This is because preventing a majority voter bloc from having a majority party is obviously undemocratic and therefore "intolerable" (Rae 1967: 75). The only feasible idea would be dividing up any potential majority voter blocs through an electoral system that is friendly to small parties.

No effort has been spared by political scientists in studying how electoral systems affect party systems. In a large number of works representing what is known as the Duvergerian agenda, the literature has repeatedly verified the statistical patterns between electoral proportionality and party system fragmentation, a rare consensus in political science being taught in the classrooms around the world. However, despite the agreement on its existence, scholars are still skeptical about whether that causal relationship can translate into clear-cut predictions that are useful for real-world institutional design.

It is repeatedly argued in the literature that when an electoral system is proportional, the fate of small parties is still conditional on whether the number of social cleavages is sufficiently large. Duverger (1959 [1951]) himself argues that despite the empirical coincidence of PR and multipartism, "On the whole P.R. maintains almost intact the structure of parties existing at the time of its appearance" (252). Grumm (1958) states, "P.R. is a result rather than a cause of the party system in a given country" (375). In addition, Lipset and Rokkan's (1967: 50) famous "freezing thesis" states that "the party systems of the 1960s reflect, with few but significant exceptions, the cleavage structures of the 1920s," which also in a way implies that institutions cannot create cleavages from nowhere, at least based on the European experience up to the mid-1960s. The most widely cited branch of the field is a series of large-N studies on electoral system effects, all of which refrain from asserting causal connections between proportionality and multipartism. Amorim Neto and Cox (1997: 167) state, "A polity can tend toward bipartism either because it has a strong electoral system or because it has few cleavages." As Clark and Golder (2006: 682) phrase the point, "Absent any knowledge concerning the social pressure for the multiplication of parties, it is not possible to predict whether multiple parties will actually form in permissive electoral systems." Similarly, Singer and Stephenson (2009: 480) argue, "The effect of electoral institutions is contingent, however, upon the presence of social cleavages that generate pressures for additional parties."

However, a key problem with these statements is that they are not directly implied by their corresponding statistical analyses. The interactive effects between ethnic fragmentation and electoral systems these scholars found imply that certain cleavage structures can complicate the Duvergerian psychological effect, making voters stay in large parties even under high proportionality, but say nothing about the mechanical effects. In fact, regardless of how stubborn a country's vote distribution may be, its seat distribution is always affected by the proportionality of the electoral system because that process is mechanically guaranteed.

Moreover, even the argument that cleavage structures can undermine the Duvergerian psychological effect is rather vulnerable. As shown by Li and Shugart's (2016) replication of Clark and Golder's (2006) regression model, the widely recognized interactive effect between ethnic fragmentation and the electoral system may have been a statistical bias that resulted from coding parliamentary systems as special cases of presidential systems.[1] When running the same regression with only parliamentary systems, the coefficient on the said interaction becomes indistinguishable from zero, meaning that the electoral system effect is not conditional on ethnic fragmentation.

Taagepera (2007) developed a series of cleavage-free models, collectively called the Seat Product Model, that link a number of party system parameters under a simple electoral system with the product of its average district magnitude (M) and total number of seats (S). In terms of the largest party's seat share (s_1), he predicts that

$$s_1 = (MS)^{-1/8}$$

Taagepera's basic logic is that the existence of noninstitutional factors does not preclude the prediction of a rough range of values that a party system parameter can take based on only institutional constraints. By taking the average of the border values of a parameter's logically possible range, one can calculate an "ignorance-based" expected value for that parameter. Li and Shugart (2016) and Shugart and Taagepera (2017) later showed that the same pattern found by Taagepera can apply to a wider range of institutions and party system parameters with some slightly modified models and that the regression coefficients often match the deduced parameters to the second decimal.

These latter pieces, in contrast to the traditional interactive models, are

---

1. In Clark and Golder (2006), the effective number of presidential candidates in parliamentary systems is coded as zero. However, according to the mathematical definition of that parameter, it cannot be smaller than one.

certainly good news for institutional designers since they greatly increased the predictive accuracy of party system fragmentation without relying on cleavage variables that are hard to measure (Fearon 2003; Stoll 2008). However, they still do not directly reveal the conditions of multipartism. First, despite their models' highly stable coefficients, there are still visible deviations between individual data points and their predicted values. Such deviations are benign for cognitive purposes, just as in any statistical model. But when applying the model to actual institutional design, could these deviations result in wrong predictions about whether a majority party would exist in a specific country? Moser and Scheiner (2012) and Ferree, Powell, and Scheiner (2014) already have shown that having a plurality system is far from enough to predict district-level bipartism because of the contextual obstacles to strategic voting. Would the same logic also lead to the failure of proportional systems to create multipartism? The importance of the question makes it deserving of further verification.

Another potential threat to both the conventional and Taageperian approaches is that their methods of regressing seat distribution against electoral systems are arguably subject to the endogeneity problem warned by Grumm (1958) and Boix (1999). One can always speculate that unobserved social cleavage forces are driving both the electoral system choices and the seat distribution. Such forces are hard to verify, if they exist at all, but they cannot be logically dismissed.

In an effort to settle the controversy over whether certain electoral systems can ensure the lack of a majority party, my recent article (Li 2018) proposes a brief theory on the demand and supply of political parties, arguing that both voters and politicians have strong incentives to split a majority party when they can. Building on that theory, I elaborate in detail in this chapter why I expect highly proportional electoral systems to always be effective in eliminating majority voter blocs, and consequently in eliminating majority parties, which suggests an optimistic view of using institutional design to address minority interests. The data analysis in the next chapter shows that there are some exceptions to the proposition, but the general pattern is reliable enough to be used by designers of political institutions.

Logical Conditions under which a Majority Party Can Exist in a Proportional Electoral System

Before discussing whether a majority party can exist in a proportional electoral system, I first lay out the logically necessary preconditions for such a party.

First, if the electoral system is highly proportional, the largest seat share should not be too different from the largest vote share, which means that we should seldom observe a "manufactured majority" (Rae 1967). It is certainly wrong to say that proportional systems never overrepresent large parties. But the cases in which a minority group is overrepresented enough to enjoy a majority of seats should be small-probability exceptions instead of commonly expected phenomena.[2]

In other words, under a commonly understood proportional electoral system, a party cannot just rely on overrepresentation to earn its majority status regularly. If a party aims to have a majority of seats, it has to work on earning a majority of votes. So when we talk about majority parties under proportional electoral systems, we are essentially referring to parties with a majority voter bloc. The conditions for a majority party in this context can be understood interchangeably as conditions for a majority voter bloc.

What, then, are needed for a majority of voters to vote for the same party? We need to approach this question from both the demand side and the supply side. On the demand side, if a majority of voters is willing to stay unified and ignore internal cleavages in the electoral field, a majority party will exist. On the supply side, if all the competent politicians that represent a majority group are willing to stay unified and refrain from offering other feasible party alternatives, a majority party will exist.

Note that these two conditions do not have to be met at the same time for a majority party to exist. As long as voters are unified, defecting politicians will not have a market. As long as politicians are unified, discontented voters will not be able to find alternative suppliers of parties. Either one of these conditions should be sufficient for the existence of a majority party. However, do they, or does either of them, exist? I show in the rest of this chapter that both the demand-side condition and the supply-side condition are very hard to maintain under a proportional electoral system and therefore majority parties are a very rare species in countries with such systems.

---

2. One might argue that there are countries that use a party list system but still create a manufactured majority regularly. Turkey and Greece are probably the most prominent examples. However, not all party list systems can be considered proportional in nature. The Greek electoral system, albeit having a proportional formula, grants 40 additional seats to the largest party, which creates a highly disproportional outcome. The Turkish system does not reward the largest party, but it imposes an extremely high threshold (10 percent of national votes, the highest in the world) to winnow out small parties. When scholars such as Lijphart and McGann recommend a proportional electoral system, they are certainly not referring to these types of systems. In this chapter, therefore, I use the term *proportional systems* to refer to those under which proportionality applies to both large and small parties, namely, MMP, medium- and large-magnitude PR, and single transferable vote (STV).

The Demand-Side Condition for a Majority Split

I first focus on the demand side of the story: whether a majority of voters will be willing to stay unified. Since this book is concerned with divided societies, sometimes called conflict-prone societies (Reilly 2006), which according to the literature (Horowitz 1985, 2002; Rabushka and Shepsle 1972; Reilly 2004) are most likely dominated by ascriptive cleavages, I only discuss majority voter blocs that are defined by an ascriptive identity.

It may be argued that a nonascriptive cleavage could also be unidimensional and result in a unified national majority. I argue in the next chapter in detail why this is logically impossible. But for now I leave this question aside because the literature rarely considers a nonascriptive majority to be truly dangerous. Whether it can survive high proportionality is therefore of less concern.

If a majority voter bloc is defined by an ascriptive identity, whether that block would prefer to split can boil down to two questions.

1. How likely is it for a majority group to share the same preference in every policy or valence judgment? In other words, can any policy combination make everyone in the majority group happy?
2. When voters within the majority disagree, how likely are they to be willing to split their support at the expense of unity? In other words, how likely are unhappy voters concerned with other cleavages to stay loyal to the original majority party?

The first question is relatively simple. The complexity of human society dictates that there has to be more than one salient cleavage in any substantial community. This is essentially a point made by Madison in Federalist Paper 10 (Madison 2003 [1787]) regarding "large republics." Chandra (2005) shows that very often a single voter can choose to identify himself with different ascriptive groups based on criteria such as race, religion, language, or caste. Even for a majority group that is both ethnically and religiously homogeneous, one can always observe conflicting interests between rural and urban residents, capital and labor, coastal and inland areas, exporters and import-substitution industries, and so on (for examples, see Lipset 1981: 230; Caramani 2004: 154). To make things even more complicated, there often exist postmaterialist cleavages (Inglehart 1977) such as those over gender equality, gay rights, and environmental issues. The crosscutting nature of these cleavages means that they divide the electorate into many different combinations of issue positions. When a party takes a specific combination of positions, it certainly satisfies only a small share of the voters.

Just answering the first question is certainly insufficient for those who believe in primordial ethnic conflict. When presenting their bipolarity models, Horowitz (1985) and Rabushka and Shepsle (1972) specifically assume that the voters within the majority group share the same preferences. As Chandra (2005) points out, they do not try to justify such an assumption but simply use it as a starting point in their models. But their implicit argument is that the primordial hostility is so strong that the opposing groups simply forget about all other conflicting interests around them. They treasure the control of the government by their coethnics so much that they vote for the existing governing party regardless of its within-group policies.

Such a view can be interpreted as another form of strategic voting. The traditional Duvergerian strategic voting focus on the district level, predicting that voters in a small district will discard parties that are not likely to win the seat to avoid wasted votes. But the same logic may apply at the national level even under a proportional system, where certain voters could discard their favorite party in fear that the minority would take advantage of the split. It could be argued that the primordial rivalry is so strong that the majority group values its unity more than the sincere expression of internal disagreements.

I agree with Horowitz (1985) and Rabushka and Shepsle (1972) that if "ethnic census voting" (Horowitz 1985) exists for a majority group, all the unfavorable outcomes they predict are likely to happen. However, is such an assumption justifiable? Can we observe the same level of ethnic voting in a majority group as much as in minority groups given a proportional electoral system?

It may not be a problem to use the above voting behavior as a premise at the beginning of the game. However, it is important to see that voters' voting strategies are endogenous to their outcomes. The tragic conclusions that Horowitz (1985) and Rabushka and Shepsle (1972) deduce from their models may affect the next round of voting and invalidate the original unification assumption.

The most important implication Horowitz (1985) and Rabushka and Shepsle (1972) draw from their bipolarity models is that the majority party will always win the election because the ascriptive identities are by definition stable. The majority party therefore has no incentive to make concessions to the minority group. Supposedly the members of the majority group should be content because, according to both models, they all share the same preference, which is on one of the far ends of the only cleavage dimension. If this is true, of course, the minority group will have no hope of improving its status unless it resorts to extrainstitutional means. It may further trigger the credible commitment problem modeled by Fearon (1998) and result in escalation of conflict.

However, there is another side effect of the model that these scholars have ignored. When there is no power alternation, even the majority group loses the ability to hold the governing party accountable. The within-majority accountability in this context implies two aspects. First, the policy position of the governing party regarding the within-majority distribution should be close to the median voter within the majority group (policy accountability). Second, the competence measure of top politicians should be higher than other alternatives within the majority group (valence accountability).

For the purpose of this chapter, there is no need to distinguish between the two types of accountability. All we need to know is that the incentive for the governing party to serve even its core constituency is weak. This side effect implies that having its own party in power may be a bad idea for the majority group itself, not just for the minority. Anticipating such effects, the initial voting behavior of the majority voters may be different from what Horowitz (1985) and Rabushka and Shepsle (1972) assume it to be. In order to hold the majority leaders accountable, they may have to give their votes to opposition parties within the majority group, even at the risk of benefiting the minority.

It may be argued that even if there is a dominant party voters can still hold politicians accountable as long as there are primary elections or an electoral system that encourages intraparty competition such as open-list proportional representation (OLPR) and single transferable vote (STV) systems.[3] Whether these institutions can encourage a majority to vote for the same party is another question I discuss later. But enforcing accountability through intraparty competition will necessarily create a demand for factions within the majority party because voters need more information than a party label to distinguish the majority partisans. Therefore, even if a majority group finds an effective way to hold its party accountable without voting for other parties, it at least needs to make that party factious and bear with the same cyclical scenario as under a fragmented party system. In

---

3. Although they are theoretically possible, majority parties under these systems are empirically rare if they exist at all.

other words, accountability requires competition and competition requires fragmentation of political forces (be they parties or factions).

In addition, there is reason to believe that intraparty competition is less effective for the following reasons, which further make additional parties preferable to factions. First, the candidates in any intraparty competition, except in highly factionalized parties, must be nominated by the existing party establishment. It is not hard to guess how much the organizers would want to see a status quo change. Party leaders may be able to manipulate who can appear on an open list or the procedure in any intraparty primary. Hazan and Rahat (2010: 27–28) argue that it is quite common for parties to allow incumbents who would like to run to get on the list either automatically or by overcoming insignificant hurdles. Even for parties that do not have such full protection for their incumbents, as Gallagher (1988: 249) observes, "the great majority survive nonetheless." The organizational protection of the incumbents simply makes it very hard for voters to hold a party accountable by altering its internal hierarchy. In contrast, incumbents cannot manipulate the ballots of other parties because the latter belong to completely different organizations and would not depend on the incumbents' mercy to be nominated.

Second, in multiparty elections, opposition groups are not in a hierarchical relationship with the incumbents and therefore are free to attack them with whatever negative campaign tactics they see fit. Attacking one's copartisans, however, is much more tricky. A challenger has to identify the incumbent's personal flaws without discrediting his party label (the most convenient information shortcut associated with him).

In sum, from a rational choice perspective, a dominant party system with a unified governing party is often not a stable equilibrium under democracy because voters lack an effective mechanism through which to reveal hidden information about the governing politicians or to hold them accountable for policy disasters. A discontented faction in a majority group either has to vote for a second party within that group or a politically salient faction within the governing party in order to gain any control over politicians.

Of course, as the last two chapters have shown, destabilizing a winning coalition means increasing the bargaining power of the minority. Whether or not to split politically is therefore a tradeoff for members of the majority group, as shown in table 7. There are two potential threats to the majority group in a dominant party system. One is losing the distributive battle against the other part of the electorate, the minority group(s). The other is losing control of their agent, the governing party. Then what we need to think about is which failure is more likely to be fatal.

For a rational voter, is it more important to hold politicians accountable or to make sure minorities have no bargaining power? I argue that the former is obviously more important. The disutility of political equality, if any, for the majority group is limited to a certain range. Under a normal democratic system, as long as the electoral process stays intact, the minority group can never be as powerful as the majority group by definition. Therefore the majority as a whole can always ensure that the minority will not dominate state resources even though the latter has proportional bargaining power. The worst thing a majority could expect is no more than sharing state resources with the minority proportionally. However, if the politicians become unaccountable, there will be no upper bound for the disutility that may be incurred by the majority group. The governing party leaders can control the party through its internal hierarchy and essentially monopolize resources for their small ruling circles. The importance of controlling political agents compared to controlling the minority is a result of the special powers of the state apparatus, including its concentrated resources, its ability to coordinate its actions, its possession of sophisticated weapons, and so on. Any rational voter, given basic information access and voting choices, will not want to see a permanent ruler.

It could be argued that clientelistic policies common in developing countries can serve as a way to maintain the popularity of a dominant party without resorting to accountability. However, clientelistic benefits, such as public sector jobs and subsidies, by definition are scarce resources and can cover only a small part of a national majority group. Those who fail to receive such benefits will still have an incentive to form new parties or factions in order to compete for patronage. In other words, even though clientelism can help politicians evade accountability, it cannot free them from competition.[4]

TABLE 7. Tradeoff between Fragmentation and Unification for a Majority Group

	Bargaining Power against Minorities	Ability to Hold the Government Accountable
Stay unified	High	Low
Support different parties	Low	High

4. The Mexican case may be a counterexample in which clientelism seems to have kept the PRI in power for 70 years. However, it would not have been so effective without the help of electoral fraud. As Magaloni (2006: 46) notes, "Every ruling party politician who split from the PRI in 1940, 1946, 1952 and 1988 alleged electoral fraud."

Of course, there is an even more common way for a party to stay dominant, which is simply abolishing the electoral provisions and divorcing itself from the principal-agent relationship with the voters. This kind of dominance is certainly not something that proportional electoral systems can directly tackle. However, it is not a phenomenon particularly associated with an ascriptively divided society but a moral hazard problem to which any type of principal agent relationship is vulnerable. There is a large literature dealing with democratic breakdowns (Linz and Stepan 1978; Cheibub et al. 1996; Cheibub 2007; Maeda 2010; Svolik 2015), which is well beyond the scope of this study. I instead limit the sample to the set of countries in which the electoral process is relatively established and can only be threatened by conflict within the electorate.

Are there any exceptional circumstances, then, under which voters would be willing to take the risk of losing control over politicians just to ensure the unity of the majority party? It is very unlikely unless the utility function of the majority voters is heavily affected by their fear of minority power. For a majority to fear a minority is certainly unusual, especially within a democracy. But it is not impossible when one or both of the following conditions exist. first, there exists a sizable minority group that controls more resources, such as wealth and human capital, than the majority group does; and, second, the minority has a history of ruling with ascriptively based oppressive policies. Logically, these two conditions tend to coincide. If the minority has never been the ruling class and discriminated against the majority, it will not have been able to accumulate much more wealth and receive significantly more education. As I show in the next chapter, this explains why South Africa is such a sharp outlier in terms of majority stability.

The Supply-Side Condition for Majority Split

In the last section, I presented a theory predicting that voters in a majority group will not be satisfied with having just one unified party even if they care about one cleavage more than other cleavages. It is in their interest to see more parties (or subparty political forces) competing within the majority group so that the politicians can be held accountable.

However, voter preferences are not the only explanatory factors of party fragmentation even under proportional systems. The strategic choices of politicians are also important. It is arguable that few politicians want to take the risk of joining a new party because their current seats are safe. Voters therefore will not have feasible alternative parties to choose from even though they would like one. In other words, politicians may not want to be held accountable. The politicians may have incentives to resist the status quo changes of a party system that may subject them to more electoral uncertainty. Therefore, in order to find out whether majority parties can be sustained under high electoral proportionality, we also need to model what politicians' preferences are.

In this section, I argue that politicians also contribute to the instability of the majority party. Because of the scarcity of legislative seats and higher appointments within a legislature compared to the supply of politicians, political newcomers and lower-ranked legislators within the majority group all have incentives to introduce additional within-group cleavages in order to increase the job turnover of political officeholders.

Assume that at a certain point in history a party enjoys a majority of national votes because a single salient cleavage dominates the society. Also assume that the country has a proportional electoral system, which means that smaller parties are not significantly underrepresented in the legislature. As I argued in the previous section, the majority group has a tendency to express other, less salient cleavages by splitting its members votes. They will not vote for the main opposition parties because their identity is so salient, but they are ready to listen to pleas from an opposition party within their group.

The founders of such an opposition party can come from two possible sources: persons outside the legislature who plan to start political careers or existing majority legislators who are dissatisfied with the status quo for whatever reason. Let me model the two scenarios separately.

(1) The Partisan Choice of Political Newcomers

What would an outsider do if he planned to start a political career in my hypothetical political system? I have assumed that there is a proportional electoral system and a strong party that monopolizes the votes of the majority group. Suppose this person is also from the majority group. He then faces two choices in terms of partisan strategy. He can either join the existing majority party or start a new party that also claims to represent the majority group. Proportional systems include several different subtypes, which imply different strategies for politicians. They need to be discussed separately.

Let me first consider a country with a closed-list proportional representation (CLPR) system. A newcomer could choose to join the existing dominant party. As mentioned previously, it is a common practice for parties to allow their incumbents to keep running. Unless an incumbent is retiring or moving on a nonlegislative job, finding a safe slot for a newcomer on the party list can be hard. If the number of newcomers is much larger than the number of leaving incumbents, some of the newcomers will have to be ranked at the bottom of their districts' lists, which means the chance that they will be elected, let alone hold any significant party position, is very low. In fact, such scarcity is true for all the world's attractive jobs.

Starting a new party within the majority identity may be a better strategy if there is a sizable group of discontented majority voters. Even if only a small part of those voters defect, the original majority party could still lose a number of seats to the new party, which means the top-ranked politicians in the new party will have a better chance of being elected than they will have inside the majority party.

The same logic applies to mixed systems. If a newcomer enters the race in a single-member district, it is highly unlikely that he will succeed unless the incumbent majority party candidate retires or dies. This is because the majority's voters will not want to give the seat to the minority by splitting the votes. The best shot for a newcomer, then, is getting his name on a list. He will then face the same tradeoff as newcomers do in pure closed-list systems and will have a strong incentive to form a new party.

Of course, not every proportional system has internally determined rankings of politicians. In OLPR and single-transferable-vote systems, senior politicians can no longer depend on their rankings for job security. Even the newcomers, theoretically, will have a good chance of beating the incumbent copartisans as long as they are popular enough among voters. However, in order for a newcomer to build such popularity quickly, he will have to adopt a campaign strategy that distinguishes him from the rest of the party. Even though he does not need a new party as much as the newcomers do under closed-list PR, he still needs to undermine the unity of the winning coalition by campaigning differently and once elected by voting differently from the party mainstream. (See the extensive party unity literature on this issue, including Cain, Ferejohn, and Fiorina 1987; Carey and Shugart 1995; Mainwaring and Pérez Liñán 1997; Garman, Haggard, and Willis 2001; Carey 2009: 162). The lack of unity in turn will result in de facto fragmentation in the country that is greater than its number of parties would suggest.

In general, no matter what kind of proportional electoral systems are used, newcomers in legislative elections have a strong incentive to form new parties or factions as long as there is enough demand. This is because those who want the seats are always more numerous than the seats available. Disunity and competition serve for politicians as a mechanism to accelerate the turnover of power and spread benefits across more individuals.

(2) The Partisan Choice of Incumbents

The theory just described applies to only newcomers. However, newcomers by themselves may not be able to affect political outcomes because of the coordination problem they face. Unlike incumbent politicians within the majority party who already have a certain name recognition, challengers may have a hard time making themselves known even if their agenda is potentially attractive. They will need to coordinate campaign financing and collective image building in order to even have a chance. This is especially true in a dominant party system where the governing party can control the propaganda machine and discredit opposition groups (see the South Africa example in Ferree 2010).

In other words, even if both supply and demand for better politicians exist, the voters may not have enough information about the potential alternatives, just as a well-made consumer product may not be able to reach customers because of the difficulties of marketing.

However, the difficulties faced by opposition politicians do not mean that additional parties cannot emerge. A split of the majority's votes can be effected from within the governing party cohort (e.g., Mershon and Shvetsova [2013] have studied numerous cases of incumbent "party fission"), which tends to be more powerful than outside opposition groups. The politicians that are already holding legislative seats will not have a hard time advertising themselves since they are already known to the public. Coordination among them is also easier since they are all familiar with each other and less subject to collective action problems. All they need to do is renounce their current party affiliation and find a new party label. Of course, the ability to form a new party does not imply the willingness to do so. A theory is then needed to show whether they would ever want to form a new party.

First, I assume that there are two potential factions in the legislative cohort of the majority party. They disagree on at least one salient issue. This assumption is justifiable because of the reasons discussed previously: the complexity of any human society simply is not compatible with identical preferences in any large group. Therefore their representatives (the politicians favored by different subgroups within the majority voter bloc) should also disagree with each other. However, the politicians in different factions do not have to make their disagreements public through open defection. They can at least pretend to be a unified group if this is politically beneficial.

Second, I assume that one faction holds more attractive offices than the other faction. Such positions could be cabinet ministers, committee chairs, party whips, speakers, and so on. A majority party may try to spread the benefits by evenly distributing important positions among different potential factions. But at least the top leadership position, especially the prime ministership in a parliamentary or semipresidential system, cannot be evenly divided. The less privileged faction therefore has an incentive to equalize the bargaining power of the two factions.

Third, assume that newcomers cannot threaten the current seat distribution. If they could, as previously argued, the majority group would have split already. It is exactly because they often could not that we need to model the behavior of incumbents.

Fourth, the utility of each faction is determined by the number of its members that are elected to the legislature and by the importance of the offices its members hold once elected.

For the faction that holds the higher appointments, the best strategy is always to maintain the status quo because they are already as well off as can be in terms of their political careers. So the key factor that determines whether the majority party will split depends on the strategy of the lower-ranked faction. Next I lay out the payoffs for that faction under different party affiliation strategies.

Since newcomers do not stand a chance, as stipulated in the third assumption, both factions have safe seats if they maintain the status quo. Therefore if the lower-ranked faction splits, there will necessarily be a risk incurred in terms of its electoral performance. The reason could be that the new party label is not yet recognized by voters (Mershon and Shvetsova 2013: 36–37) or that the defection has created an image that is not credible and breaks the electoral connection (Mayhew 1974). Since the status quo means safe seats, any adjustment in strategies cannot be electorally beneficial. Pure electoral incentives do have strong explanatory power over incumbent splits in general (Mershon and Shvetsova 2013: 102), but they may be less powerful under a truly dominant party system in which electoral uncertainty is low.

However, politicians are rarely satisfied with just being elected. The payoffs from higher offices can significantly increase the total utility of a legislator. For example, some immediately available data on European countries (Macias and Nudelman 2015; Preisvergleich.de 2013) suggest that the salaries of prime ministers are normally twice as high as those of backbench legislators. Of course, more detailed data on other ministers' salaries would help us establish a better sense of politicians' office incentives. But this is enough to show that maintaining the status quo is often not the best strategy if we take into consideration the benefits of promotion. What can the lower-ranked faction do, then, to increase the turnover of high parliamentary offices? The most obvious answer is competing for them. But competition between legislators for offices can mean two things.

First, they can compete by showing their loyalty to the party. As Benedetto and Hix (2007) show, members of parliament who vote loyally with their parties are often associated with better prospects of entering the cabinet in the United Kingdom. This certainly makes sense under a Westminster system, in which the leaders of the largest party normally have monopoly power over cabinet appointments. Such a competition mechanism by definition results in slow turnover. It would be an oxymoron to say that someone replaced the leader by being loyal. Loyalty may help a backbencher get closer to the vacancy a leader left voluntarily, but normally it cannot help him defeat a leader.

Second, legislators can also compete by seeking an alternative winning coalition. Under a proportional electoral system, as long as a splinter party can find a significant number of supporters, the original majority party cannot rely on strategic voting to maintain its monopoly on legislative decisions, including within-legislature appointments. Therefore, the lower-ranked politicians in these systems have a more efficient way of accelerating office turnover, that is, taking away the legislative confidence of the current leaders.

The empirical evidence can be seen in Mershon and Shvetsova (2013: 77, 104). Party switch in general and party fission in particular are both more common under proportional systems. The frequent party splits in Italy, according to Mershon and Shvetsova, can be explained by the high likelihood that the splinters will survive. Of course, it is harder to find such a case under a dominant party system, which would be more directly relevant. That is not because dominant parties are harder to split but simply because parties do not normally have a chance to become dominant in the first place under proportional systems.

South Africa, as I discuss later, certainly is a counterexample for this theory since the dominant party there has been highly stable even under a highly proportional system. But it does support the speculation that senior majority party members have an incentive to split the party in their fight for higher offices. The African National Congress (ANC), regardless of its dominance, has experienced many cases of high-profile splitting that resulted in at least three different splinter parties.[5] None of these splits came close to bringing down the ANC's majority status. Nonetheless, they suggest that splitting is a strategy worth trying for many, and this one could have worked under a slightly less salient majority.

In sum, lower-ranked politicians in a dominant party have strong incentives to undermine their own party (even though it is permissive for small parties). Incumbent politicians may not want to see legislative seat reshuffles as much as political newcomers do, but they nonetheless have reasons to destabilize the status quo.

Conclusion

Knowing from the previous chapters that fragmentation of the winning coalition is a key explanation for minorities' bargaining power, we have to ask ourselves whether such fragmentation is always possible. Specifically, can majority parties survive high proportionality? Based on the theory provided in this chapter, it should be unlikely.

On the demand side, a majority group needs more than one party in order to hold the majority party accountable for poor performance and deviation from the majority median, which are much more important goals than staying unified against minorities. Once such parties emerge, majority voters are willing to split their votes because proportionality frees them from the threat of wasted votes.

On the supply side, political newcomers and lower-ranked politicians in a majority group are happy to run against the majority party in order to increase the turnover of legislative seats and higher positions within the legislature. Such incentives are strong because of the relative abundance of potential competitors compared to the number of available seats and offices. As long as politicians sense the demand for new parties by the electorate and believe that the electoral system will not significantly waste their votes, they will not hesitate to fragment the winning coalition.

Note that these theories do not imply that dominant parties cannot disappear for other reasons (see Stoll's [2013] social heterogeneity explanation of party system evolution) such as demographic changes, economic development, or the death of certain leaders. They are simply saying that, even

---

5. These parties are the United Democratic Movement (1997), Congress of the People (2008), and Economic Freedom Fighters (2013).

if all other conditions are absent, an ascriptive majority party will cease to exist under proportional systems just because it is not a stable equilibrium.

It is hard to test these party split mechanisms directly because dominant parties under proportional systems are simply too rare to support a meaningful dataset. However, such rareness itself may be an indicator of the effectiveness of my theories. In the next chapter I offer a test of these ideas using the largest parties' vote share data.

SEVEN

Verifying the Electoral System Effect on Splitting Majorities

In the last chapter, I introduced a theory predicting that rarely can a party win a majority of votes under a proportional system based on both the demand and the supply of new parties, which implies that majority parties will also be rare as long as the largest seat share is sufficiently close to the largest vote share, which is normally the case under proportional electoral systems.

I test the theory in two general steps. First, I show that majority voter blocs are a rare species in the electoral world. In very few countries does a majority party actually receive a majority of votes. Second, I show that in the few countries where a majority voting bloc does exist, usually this bloc is actually a strategic coalition of disagreeing groups and will most likely split given high proportionality.

I also provide a detailed discussion of key outliers, such as South Africa, explaining why they are so different from the rest of the world.

A Typology of Majority Parties

The ultimate question I want to answer in this chapter is how confident we can be that a majority party will cease to exist in a country in which a highly proportional electoral system is adopted. In order to answer this question, let us first look at a typology of majority parties according to their corresponding support bases (table 8).

First, when a party attracts only a minority of votes but wins a majority of seats because of disproportionality, it is defined by Rae (1967) as a "manufactured majority." This type of majority party can be easily identified by looking at its vote share. If the largest party's vote share is smaller than 0.5, we can confidently predict that its seat share will also be smaller than 0.5 when the seat share is proportional to the vote share.

One could argue that the largest vote share cannot be held constant across different electoral systems. It is certainly true that the largest party share may change in response to proportionality, but the direction of that change is restrained. Because of the Duvergerian psychological effect, the vote concentration should decrease but not increase when the system becomes more proportional. If the largest party cannot gain 50 percent of the votes under a majoritarian electoral system, it will almost never be able to do so under a proportional system.[1] Combined with the mechanical effects of proportionality, we can say that the same party will likely be unable to earn more than 50 percent of the seats.

New Zealand, prior to electoral reform, was very typical of systems that frequently see this kind of majority party. One policy consequence was that radical policies resulted from unchecked majority parties that took turns controlling the government while each winning a minority of the votes

TABLE 8. A Typology of Majority Parties

Term	Definition	Unified Majority of Voters?	Result under High Proportionality
Manufactured majority	A majority party voted for only by a minority of voters.	No	Majority party would not exist
Earned majority			
Sincere majority	A majority party sincerely voted for by a majority of voters.	Yes	Majority party would still exist
Strategic majority	A majority party voted for by a majority of voters, but sincerely voted for only by a minority.	No	Majority party would not exist

---

1. Theoretically, there could certainly be exceptions in which parties choose to merge after switching from a majoritarian to a proportional system for various reasons. For example, small parties may want to merge to get around a legal threshold. But such exceptions are rare enough for us to safely assume that the largest vote share does decrease with proportionality.

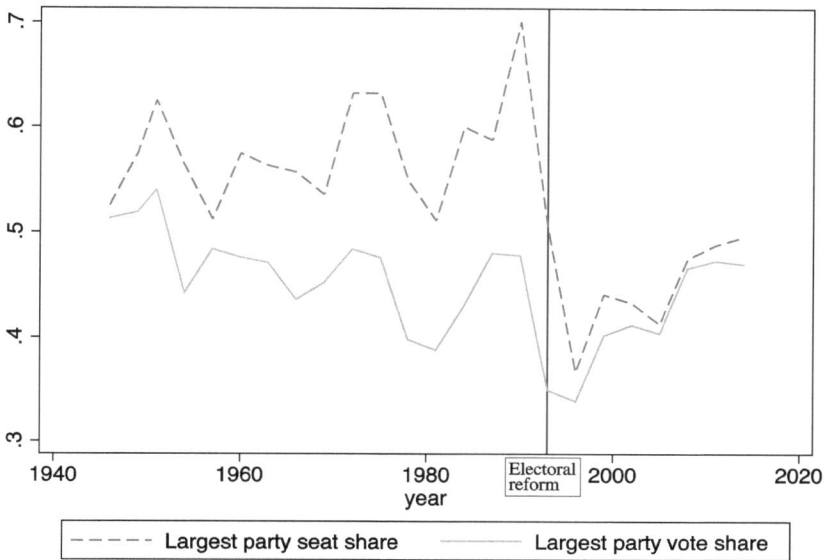

Fig. 7. The New Zealand party system before and after electoral reform

(Bollard 1994; Nagel 1994). Although New Zealand was not the kind of typical divided society with which this book is mainly concerned, it did have a problem similar to those of unidimensional societies: an overconcentration of power in the two alternating governing parties. From an institutional design perspective, this type of overconcentration of power can be effectively remedied by increasing proportionality, which is what New Zealand successfully did, starting with the 1996 election, under a mixed-member proportional system. As can be seen in figure 7, since the two alternating majority parties in New Zealand rarely earned more than 50 percent of the votes, their seat shares also fell below 50 percent immediately after the electoral reform.

In contrast, if a majority party truly receives more than half the votes, it is defined by Rae (1967) as an "earned majority." Since this term does not tell us whether the majority of votes received by that party reflects the true social cleavages, I further divide this type into two smaller ones, as discussed below.

If a majority party is supported by a majority of voters sincerely, which likely is the case in South Africa, where the majority is loyal to the ANC even when small parties are proportionally represented, I call it a sincere majority. If power concentration becomes a problem in such a case, one obviously cannot rely on the same institutional solution employed in New Zealand because the electoral systems were already as friendly to small parties as could be. As Rae (1967: 75) notes, "It would be intolerable" for any electoral system to give a minority of seats to a dominant majority voter bloc.[2] In order to constrain the largest party, a country like South Africa might have to adopt certain supermajority rules in legislative decision making or wait until its social cleavage structure evolves beyond its historical legacy.

In contrast, there may also be cases in which the majority party does have a majority of votes but the voters vote that way only because of the Duvergerian strategic concern. The majority voter bloc is essentially a strategic coalition of different groups that have salient internal disagreements. Making electoral systems more permissive might also be a good idea for these countries when the power concentration becomes high enough to pose a threat. Even though their majority parties seem highly popular, voters will likely defect when small parties are given a greater chance of surviving, just like what I modeled in the previous chapter.

One cannot distinguish between the latter two types of majority parties just by looking at the vote share data because in both scenarios the largest party has more than half of the votes. However, we can rely on other clues to tell them apart, which I discuss in detail in later sections. For now all we need to know is that sincere majorities are the only type of majority parties that can survive proportionality. Therefore, in order to decide how effective proportionality is as a mechanism to protect minorities through cycling, we need to find out how frequently earned majorities exist and among them how frequently sincere majorities exist in the world's democracies.

The Data

In order to identify the different kinds of majority voter blocs, I collected all available data on the largest parties' vote shares (first round and lower house only) in postwar legislative elections through 2015 from countries around the world, excluding microstates that lack a Polity score. For most of the analyses I present, I include only elections that happened when the

---

2. Cases in which a party earns a majority of votes but not a majority of seats occasionally occur because of malapportionment, but this is never the outcome that institutional designers want.

Polity score of the country was six or higher so that the conclusion would not be affected by the cases of vote concentration that result from electoral fraud or intimidation of voters. I also dropped countries that had only three or fewer elections in order to prevent the results from being driven by disequilibrium conditions in very young democracies. There are, in total, 83 countries that satisfy my condition of inclusion. I address the possible problems associated with case selection in later sections, discussing additional democracies that had a shorter life span or less established institutions.

The largest vote share and electoral system data are from Nohlen and Stover (2010); Nohlen, Grotz, and Hartmann (2001); Nohlen, Krennerich, and Thibaut (1999); Nohlen (2005); Bormann and Golder (2013); Carr (n.d.); and Carey and Hix (2011). Executive-type data are from Robbers (2007); Bormann and Golder (2013); and Li and Shugart (2016). Democracy scores are from Marshall, Jaggers, and Gurr (2014). While I was revising this book, two colleagues and I combined its data into an upcoming party system dataset with both national and district levels, which will be ready to download shortly (Struthers, Li, and Shugart 2018).

The Rarity of Earned Majorities

The first step is relatively easy. All we need to do is to find out how frequently majority voter blocs exist. Rae (1967) has some initial tests regarding how rare the majority voter blocs are. He finds that 16 out of all 117 elections (13.7 percent) in his dataset see an "earned majority." This is certainly indicative of the rarity of majority voter blocs, but it is by no means as striking as the real-world situation for two reasons. First, Rae has only a small set of data consisting of only 20 countries (including very small states such as Luxembourg and Iceland) with only a few elections in each country, which is poorly representative of the rest of the world, especially newer democracies (considering that Rae's sample of countries was assembled half a century ago). Second, he does not emphasize between-country variations when presenting his results. Since the within-country variations in a short time period are more likely to result from short-term political events and do not reflect the underlying cleavage structure or institutional constraints in a country, they are less useful for general institutional studies.

In this section, I perform a long-deserved upgrade to Rae's test by employing a much larger dataset and focusing on between-country variations. My dependent variable, therefore, will be whether a country tends to

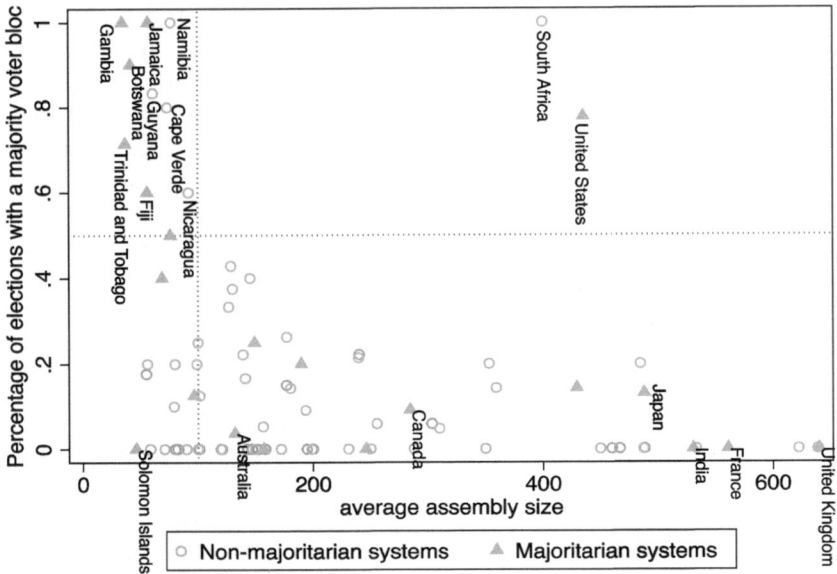

Fig. 8. Frequency of majority voter blocs under different electoral systems

have a majority voter bloc. I define a country as having such a tendency if majority voter blocs appear in more than half of its lower house elections.[3]

The most important explanatory variable is certainly the type of electoral system. But, as elaborated in Taagepera (2007), the size of the legislature also plays an important role in restricting party fragmentation. In figure 8, the assembly size is indicated by the horizontal axis while the electoral formula is captured by the shape of the data points.[4] Nonmajoritarian systems include any country that has a proportional tier in its electoral system in most of its elections.

A striking observation is immediately visible in the figure. Not only is the number of countries that tend to have a majority voter bloc quite small

3. There is only one ambiguous country in the dataset, Honduras, where exactly half the elections produced a majority party. However, its most recent election, which is outside the coverage of the data period, saw an extremely fragmented party system with the largest vote share amounting to 36.9 percent. I therefore categorize it as a country without a majority voter bloc on average.

4. The variation within PR systems, especially that of district magnitude, certainly makes a lot of difference. However, since this chapter is more concerned with the binary outcome of whether a majority group exists, and since there is already a large literature on district magnitude, I retain only the most relevant factors in the graph.

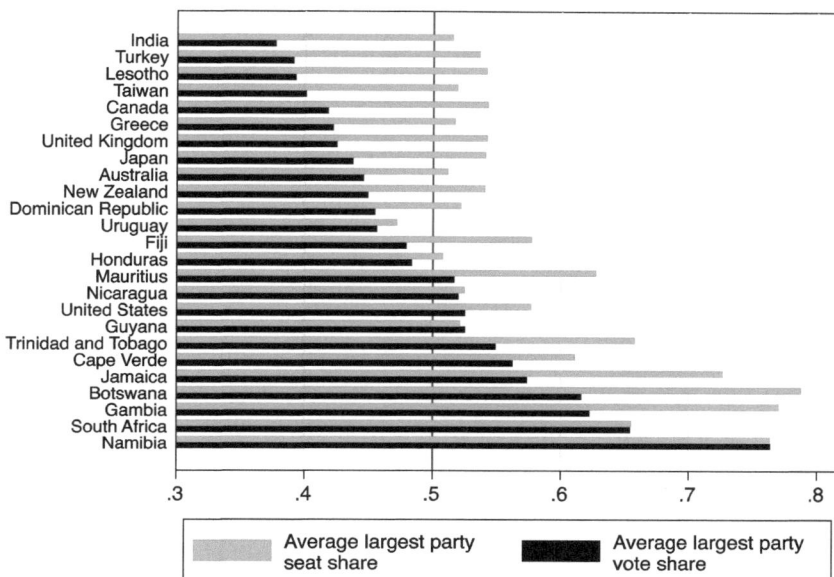

Fig. 9. Comparing largest party vote share and largest party seat share in 25 majoritarian democracies

(11 out of 83, or 13.3 percent), but they are mostly crowded on the far left side of the graph. This means that majority voter blocs are especially rare in countries with large legislatures (2 out of 60 countries in which the average assembly size is 100 or higher). I labeled a few countries in this group that are considered typical majoritarian party systems, including Japan, Canada, and the United Kingdom. The data show that their majority parties rarely if ever won a majority of the popular votes. Even a once dominant party such as the Indian National Congress never reached a popular vote majority.

Another way of looking at the phenomenon is through figure 9, which contrasts the largest parties' average seat shares and vote shares in the 25 countries that normally have a majority legislative party. It appears that most of these countries' majority parties greatly depend on mechanical disproportionality to maintain their majority status. On average, the boost given to the largest parties by the electoral systems in these countries is about 9 percent of the total seats.

Before going into any country details, we can already conclude that most of the democracies in the dataset (72 out of 83 countries) do not tend to have a majority voter bloc. One can conclude with full confidence that these 72 countries would not have a majority party regularly had they adopted highly proportional electoral systems.

Sincere Majorities versus Strategic Majorities

Simply knowing that majority voter blocs are rare is important, but it is far from enough for the purpose of verifying the effectiveness of proportional systems. There are still 11 democracies, including the United States, that do tend to have majority voter blocs. What can we say about these countries? What if a divided society an institutional engineer is working on happens to bear similarities to these 11 democracies? How confident are we that a proportional system can cure its overconcentration of power?

Even in a country that does have a majority voter bloc, that bloc may be a strategic coalition that would easily dissolve were the electoral system more proportional. There are three ways to discern this type of unstable voter bloc, as summarized in figure 10 and explained below.

The first is the majority alternation criterion. If a country's majority vote winners alternate across elections, this implies that no party has a core constituency as large as a national majority. A party's ability to win a majority of votes must be dependent on a large number of swing voters. For the purposes of this chapter, we do not have to go into the detailed characteristics of core and swing voters (Cox and McCubbins 1986). All we need to know is that they are different. In a given election, a party's core and swing voters may share certain preferences that unite them. But by definition they must disagree on other salient dimensions, be they economic, ascriptive, or normative, without which they would not have voted differently in other elections.

The second is the electoral system criterion. Even if a country is dominated by a single majority voter bloc, we cannot yet conclude that the dominant party can survive increased proportionality. It is possible that the supporters of such a party are held together by the Duvergerian psychological effect. Once the electoral constraints on small parties are removed, they could disaggregate into smaller groups that support different parties. It is much harder to detect such psychological effects than it is to detect pure mechanical effects because the vote share data alone do not reveal why voters vote a certain way. In such cases, we have to resort to a traditional comparative approach to see whether the dominant majority voter blocs coincide with more restrictive electoral systems. Such a method, just like the conventional approach, can be vulnerable to the risk of endog-

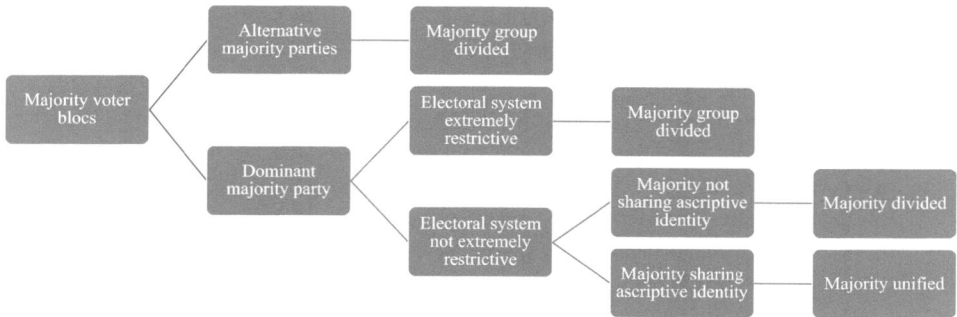

Fig. 10. Steps taken to identify unified majority groups

enous institutions. However, I show in the next section that the reversed causal direction is highly unlikely for the few countries that require cross-national comparison. These countries happen to have electoral systems that are exceedingly disproportional, with not only a plurality formula but also some of the smallest assembly sizes in the dataset. The extremity of these systems makes their effects hard to dismiss.

The third is the ascriptive majority criterion. What if a dominant majority voter bloc exists under an electoral system with only moderate restrictiveness? Is there a way to tell whether the electoral system or the inherent cleavages are responsible? Another helpful criterion is whether the majority voter bloc possesses a clear ascriptive identity, claiming itself as a racial, ethnic, linguistic, or religious group. If not, we should not expect such a group to maintain unity under highly proportional electoral systems because the strategic need for unity would no longer exist.

It may be possible for the "working class" to serve as an alternative identity to keep a majority voter bloc together. However, a class-based coalition is by no means stable for a few reasons. Most important, economic identities are more fluid and ambiguous and therefore cannot serve as an "information shortcut" like ethnic identities do (Chandra 2007). A worker in an import-substitution industry may benefit from a labor movement at the expense of his employer, but he may also benefit from a protectionist policy at the expense of consumers. The quantifiable nature of monetary benefits implies that a rational worker does not care which source contributes to those benefits but only about the quantity. So he can easily transfer from one ad hoc coalition to another depending on the marginal benefits that accrue from his vote. Therefore, we rarely observe stable majorities based on pure economic cleavages. Second, pure economic identities are not likely to coincide with primordial conflicts as in ascriptively divided societies (Rabushka and Shepsle 1972: 8). Pure economic status can certainly be hereditary, but it is hard to trace most of the personal wealth in modern societies back to centuries earlier because of frequent regime changes and social transformations unless such wealth is correlated with other, more stable and visible identities such as race and religion. And, finally, nonethnic identities are often crosscut by ethnic ones and suffer internal divisions (Horowitz 1985: 298–302). Even if there exists a salient "class" identity, different ethnic groups within that class can be expected to have very different policy preferences. This is exactly why electoral system scholars, including Cox (1997), Clark and Golder (2006), Ordeshook and Shvetsova (1994), and Stoll (2008), choose to use ethnic or religious diversity, instead of economic factors, to proxy the number of cleavages.

In sum, we should expect a dominant party to survive regardless of high proportionality only if the three criteria are met at the same time: (1) there normally exists a majority voter bloc that does not alternate between parties; (2) the original electoral system is not exceptionally restrictive; and (3) the majority voter bloc shares an ascriptive identity. Below I identify the countries that meet any or all of these conditions and explain what the results imply. Next I use these criteria to detect whether majority voter blocs in the 11 countries that tend to have them reflect unified identities or ad hoc coalitions. The small number of such cases allows me to use an exhaustive approach, listing all the relevant factors in table 9.

In table 9, the second column indicates whether a country's popular vote winner alternates across elections. The third and fourth columns indicate some key institutional components of these countries. In the last column, I calculated a best guess of their largest parties' sizes based on their institutional variables alone using the Seat Product Model.[5]

The countries in rows 1 through 6 frequently have majority voter blocs, but they alternate between different parties. Guyana's People's Progressive Party was dominant for two decades but eventually lost the 2015 election by a small margin. In the other five countries, the number of swing voters is much larger. It can be said that no single stable identity can claim a majority in these countries. When their electoral systems are made more proportional, with either a larger assembly size or a larger district magnitude, we should expect their majority parties to split.

The countries in rows 5 through 9, including the two that overlap with

---

5. The largest seat shares in simple electoral systems are calculated based on $s_1 = (MS)^{-1/8}$ (Taagepera 2007). South Africa's compensatory two-tier system cannot be predicted directly from the model.

the last group, share extremely restrictive electoral systems, namely, single-member plurality systems with very small assembly sizes. Note in figure 8 that these countries' data points show that they have some of the smallest assemblies among all majoritarian electoral systems in the sample. Consequently, the institutional constraints alone already predict a very comfortable majority party (column 5 of table 9) even when all other information is missing. Considering that majority voter blocs are extremely rare in other countries, theirs would most likely not exist if their electoral systems were moved from the restrictive end to the proportional end.

Now we are left with the only two dominant party systems that coincide with high proportionality. South Africa distributes 400 legislative seats proportionally according to parties' national vote shares. Its two-tiered PR system is one of the most proportional systems in the world. Although Taagepera's model does not provide a direct formula for two-tier systems, we can safely assume that the South African system is no less permissive than a list PR system with a similar assembly size and basic-tier district magnitude. Its former colony, Namibia, has a comparably proportional system of PR with one national district. Nonetheless, the two countries' largest parties both have stable support of around two-thirds of the voters without the help of any institutional forces. It is notable that the highly proportional systems in the two countries were accepted by their respective dominant parties, the ANC and SWAPO (South West African People's

TABLE 9. Identifying Stable Majority Groups in 11 Countries with Majority Voter Blocs

Country	Popular Vote Winner Alternation	Average Assembly Size	Electoral System	Seat Product Model Prediction of Largest Seat Share	Stable Majority Group
1. United States	**Yes**	435	Plurality	0.47	No
2. Cape Verde	**Yes**	73.4	PR	0.49	
3. Nicaragua	**Yes**	92	PR	0.46	
4. Guyana	**Yes**	61	PR	0.47	
5. Trinidad and Tobago	**Yes**	**36.6**	Plurality	**0.64**	
6. Jamaica	**Yes**	**56.8**	Plurality	**0.6**	
7. Gambia (1966–92)	No	**34.3**	Plurality	**0.64**	
8. Botswana	No	**41.4**	Plurality	**0.63**	
9. Fiji (1972–82)	No	**52**	Plurality	**0.61**	
10. Namibia	No	76.8	PR	0.34	Yes
11. South Africa	No	400	Two-tier PR	N/A	

Note: The bold cells highlight why their majority groups are institutional phenomena.

Organisation), exactly as a compromise to reassure minorities about their interests under universal suffrage (Reynolds 1995), but the party system has remained persistently majoritarian.

Outliers of Different Kinds:
The United States and South Africa

Now I have identified eight countries with strategic majority voter blocs and two with a sincere majority voter bloc. In table 9, we can see that most of these countries have legislatures with less than 100 seats. Not surprisingly, they also have very small populations (see the Cube Root Law theorized in Taagepera and Shugart 1989 and empirically verified in Shugart and Taagepera 2017). I discussed many of them in the previous sections and will not go into further detail.

However, there are two prominent outliers that deserve additional attention. South Africa and the United States are the only two large countries (also with large legislatures) that constantly have majority voter blocs. As I have shown previously, they certainly cannot be explained using the same theory. South Africa has a sincere majority voter bloc that is ascriptively driven and has yet to show any sign of losing elections. The United States, however, has two alternate winning parties that are not ascriptively defined but often enjoy a majority of votes regardless. In this section, I deal with these two outliers separately and try to understand why they are so different from the rest of the world. Only by proving that the outliers are truly different can we be more confident about the general patterns found in other countries.

(1) The Legacy of Collective "Dictators" in South Africa

If the general pattern of fragmented voters can be explained by the large number of cleavages in most of the societies, it is not hard to understand why South Africa is such a big outlier.

The period of racial segregation was a unique scenario in terms of its influence on later democratic competition. Different versions of segregation were not uncommon in predemocratic history around the world, but none had a within-minority democracy as developed and formal as that in South Africa in the apartheid period. The country had a Polity score as high as four, one of the highest among countries with a small suffrage. Unlike other nondemocracies, in which the privileged ruling class is confined to a small group of people, South Africa had a much larger "selectorate,"[6] the white population as a whole. Such a unique type of inequality made a very effective campaign label for the revolutionary party after democratization. Had the ruling class been smaller and not visually distinct, as in monarchies or the former Communist states, it would have been very hard for revolutionary sentiments to stay fixed in the later democratic competition.

The South African cleavage structure, therefore, is unique in that a generation of voters grew up in an environment in which race was the single most salient social cleavage. The generational factor alone may be temporary, but the minority's disproportional wealth and human capital accumulated during the apartheid period (Bond 2014: 19–21; Butler 2009: 92) can be passed on for generations and continuously make the majority group feel threatened or at least dissatisfied.

Ferree (2010) offers a detailed analysis of how the ANC successfully labeled the main opposition party, the Democratic Alliance, as the "white party" that had been responsible for apartheid, consequently leaving African voters with no choice but to stay with the party that led the crusade for democratic change. However, Ferree does not directly explain how the ANC prevents other African parties from earning a significant share of votes. In fact the racial divide not only prevents cross-racial voting, but, more important, it causes the majority group to fear the possibility of a fragmented winning coalition of which the minority group could take advantage. Using the defection cost framework developed in chapter 3 of this book, we can say that voters are using their unified partisan choice to increase the defection costs of African politicians so that they will not undermine the current policy directions by temporarily siding with white parties. Under a highly proportional system with low institutional defection costs, the only way for voters to prevent cycling would be not voting for small parties.

It is no wonder that South Africa's former colony, Namibia, happens to be the only other obvious outlier. Its significant white population, past racial segregation policy, and white-only political representation exactly mirrored those of South Africa. The country's fight for independence from South Africa, therefore, was at the same time a struggle against apartheid. The coincidence of these two outliers suggest that their shared legacy from a significant minority's collective dictatorship very likely explains their unidimensional cleavage structures, which are rarely seen in other democracies.

---

6. "Selectorate" is a term first used by Roeder (1993) to refer to the small circle of people who select and remove leaders in authoritarian systems.

One thing to keep in mind, however, is that, although the South African party system is an outlier in terms of its unidimensional cleavage structure, its supply-side story is not much different from those of other countries. Lower-ranked politicians, as in other countries, have strong incentives to invoke secondary cleavages in order to increase job turnover. The only problem for them is that the voters, the demand side of political parties, have yet to respond actively. As shown in table 10, the ANC politicians have repeatedly attempted to build splinter parties to challenge its dominance, just as one would predict under a highly proportional system, but the voters have not shown much enthusiasm. The recent resignation of the long-serving South African president Jacob Zuma,[7] who was facing the credible threat of a no-confidence vote, further indicates the increasing division among ANC politicians. If the splitting efforts of ANC politicians continue, it is only a matter of time before the country loses its majority party.

As if political showdowns are not dramatic enough, another unique phenomenon that characterizes the ANC is its frequent assassinations, which are normally carried out by rivals within the party. Onishi and Gebrekidan (2018) report that about 90 ANC politicians have been killed since the beginning of 2016. Although these assassinations result more from corruption cover-ups than normal policy disagreements, they nonetheless show that ANC politicians are no more unified than those in other political parties around the world.

Therefore, the true reason for the stable majority status of the ANC can only come from the demand side. The voters treasure the party label too much because of its legacy of unifying nonwhite voters, so ambitious politicians have no choice but to stay under that label.

TABLE 10. Parties Formed by ANC Defectors

Election prior to the Split	Splinter Party	Vote Share of Splinter Party in First Election	ANC Vote Share Change
1997	United Democratic Movement	3.42%	3.2%
2008	Congress of the People	7.4%	−3.8%
2013	Economic Freedom Fighters	6.4%	−3.7%

7. Although the South African chief executives are known as presidents, they are equivalent to prime ministers because they are elected and can be dismissed by the parliament.

(2) Another Version of American Exceptionalism

It is also important to offer some explanations for the other significant outlier, the United States. Many theories in comparative politics are borrowed from the works on American politics because the latter is a much older discipline and enjoys much more complete and detailed data. It is a common practice for comparativists to advance their arguments by drawing from US examples (Taylor et al. 2014). However, if the United States turns out to be a case that is unique in one of the most basic dimensions of democracy, the distribution of votes, we will have to be extra careful when applying the US experience to the rest of the world.

The cleavage explanation for South Africa is not sufficient in the US case. It would be counterintuitive to argue that the United States is dominated by a single cleavage, as it is probably one of the most diverse democracies in terms of salient political topics. Bowler, Grofman, and Blais (2009: 144) suggest briefly that it may be the case that "voters may see politics in one-dimensional terms" because their positions on different policy issues are highly correlated. However, there is no empirical evidence suggesting that such correlation is stronger in the United States than in other countries. And if it is, that is even more puzzling since we do not know where such correlation comes from.

There are certainly many different versions of American exceptionalism in terms of social conditions, as summarized by Ross (1992), but none seems directly related to vote concentration. Some early Marxists viewed the United States as unique in that it lacked a disgruntled working class (Lovestone 1928). This may have contributed to the early formation of an ideologically moderate party system in the United States. But it cannot explain the country's uniqueness in the present day when the rest of the industrialized world has become no less economically equal.

One could also argue that American parties are more inclusive, but that would only beg more questions. Why are they more inclusive? Is there any institutional reason behind it or is it just a historical accident? If a party is really inclusive, can we still view it as a unified political force like a typical European party? If not, can we still say that the US is an outlier?

Therefore, it is important to not stop at the inclusiveness explanation and look for exogenous factors for vote concentration that exist only in the United States. Here I present a few potential explanations, although the current evidence is not yet enough to tell which are most important.

First, the United States is the only established democracy that combines presidentialism with a simple plurality legislative electoral system.

The plurality system by itself is not enough to create a pure two-party system because the Duvergerian effects mainly work on the district level. As can be seen in plurality systems such as those of the United Kingdom, Canada, and India, many small parties can survive as long as they manage to find concentrated regional support. In the United States, however, not only does the plurality system encourage local bipartism, but the much more eye-catching presidential elections also make regional parties hard to sustain. Any political party that tries to label itself as a Texan party or a Californian party will not have a share of the TV and internet carnivals that surround presidential elections.

Second, the United States not only has a dominant eye-catching presidency, but also the Electoral College system used in US presidential elections is not seen in other countries. As Bowler, Grofman, and Blais (2009: 135) argue, even if a party wants to earn a small portion of the Electoral College votes, it has to have concentrated support in a state. This certainly makes it hardly meaningful for any small party to even give it a try. After a strict two-party system is institutionalized in presidential elections, the suppressed parties pass to the legislative party system through "coattail effects," which results in a similar two-party system in the legislature.

Third, the Electoral College system in itself may not be decisive enough because one may argue that a popular third party could still emerge and win a certain number of Electoral College votes, resulting in an external shock to both major parties. However, the other part of the presidential electoral system makes it even harder for small parties to survive. According to the Twelfth Amendment (1804) of the US Constitution, when no presidential candidate receives an absolute majority of the Electoral College votes, the House of Representatives will choose the president. And, even more unusual, each state delegation, regardless of the size of the state, will have one vote if the House has to choose a president.

It could be argued that how a president would be chosen in this scenario is not important because it has rarely happened. However, the fact that it is unusual is itself endogenous to the electoral rules. Anticipating that they might completely lose control of the presidential election to "state delegations," voters and interest groups would necessarily try to prevent that scenario from happening in the first place. Thus, strategic voting and strategic entry in favor of large parties naturally become a rational strategy.

The 2016 US presidential election provides a very useful example. In his announcement that he would quit the presidential race, Michael Bloomberg (2016) explicitly mentioned his fear of the Twelfth Amendment.

In a three-way race, it's unlikely any candidate would win a majority of electoral votes, and then the power to choose the president would be taken out of the hands of the American people and thrown to Congress. The fact is, even if I were to receive the most popular votes and the most electoral votes, victory would be highly unlikely, because most members of Congress would vote for their party's nominee.

As popular and resourceful as Bloomberg is, he might be able to start a third-party movement even under a highly unfriendly electoral system. But the Twelfth Amendment apparently was the last straw that tipped his decision.

Finally, the United States is the only country in which direct primary elections are required for nominating legislative candidates. Such a bottom-up nomination rule, according to Taylor et al. (2014), allows politicians to distinguish themselves from others and fight over secondary cleavages through the nomination process within a party instead of having to form new parties as they would do in other countries. They argue that the Tea Party faction of the Republican Party is a good example of how politicians choose to express their differences under the same party label.

Partly as a result of such intraparty direct elections, any majority voter bloc that emerged in an American congressional election was, until very recently, far from any real ideological bloc with a clearly generalizable collective will. Such a claim may be verified by a House cross-voting rate that ranges from 10 to 30 percent since 1954 and a percentage of "party unity votes" lower than half on average (see Jacobson 2013: 261).[8] It is certainly hard to tell how significant these numbers are since there is a lack of similar data for other countries. But there are still ways to compare these numbers with those of other countries. For example, Kam (2009: 8, table 1.1) presents the percentage of "dissenting divisions" (bills in which at least one party member voted against the party majority) data of major parties in four countries: Britain, Canada, Australia, and New Zealand. It appears that in all these parties prefect unity is extremely common in parliamentary voting. Even in a less unified party, legislators vote unanimously in at least 85 percent of the divisions. In contrast, perfect unity is next to impossible in the United States. Even the so-called party unity votes are far from unanimous within party lines.

---

8. "Party unity votes" refers to votes in which majorities of Democrats and Republicans took opposite sides.

In addition, in Kam's (2009: 75–170) country-specific chapters, his data show that even in the parliamentary divisions where party dissent happened the percentages of members of parliament (MPs) who voted against their parties was almost always below 10 percent, which means the average probability that an MP will vote against his party is normally the product of two one-digit percentages, which is negligible compared to the cross-voting rate in the United States.

Another important indicator of the intraparty cleavages in the United States is the high frequency of divided government even under concurrent elections, which, according to Shugart (1995), have been rare in other presidential systems. Shugart suggests that this may be the result of the intraparty competitions that have made elections more personalized. The fact that voters often split their votes in legislative and presidential elections clearly implies that they have salient disagreements with both parties and would be happy to accept more parties whenever electoral systems allow them to emerge.

Of course, as mentioned in chapter 5, party unity in the United States has increased dramatically in recent years, especially under the Trump presidency. That may have to do with the increased polarization of parties, which sorts voters and politicians into two opposite camps (Fiorina, Abrams, and Pope 2005). But it could also simply result from the fact that parties have become more presidentialized (Samuels and Shugart 2010) under the increasing publicity of national politics, especially that of presidential compared to legislative campaigns. In other words, legislative candidates not only lack the freedom to choose smaller party labels, but they are also increasingly subordinate to their parties' presidential candidates, especially when a candidate is as adept at attracting media attention as Donald Trump. This means that congressional primary elections may become less of an arena for intraparty diversity and more of a loyalty show for the party leader. Nonetheless, such primaries still serve the purpose of allowing ambitious politicians to challenge their own parties' candidates without having to form new parties.

This analysis shows that, although the United States may be an outlier in terms of the concentration of votes in two major parties, it does conform to the general patterns in other countries in two ways.

First, although the United States does not have a small legislature, its presidential elections serve as an alternative mechanism through which to restrict the expression of cross-district cleavages. In order to enjoy a share of the presidential coattail effects under an extremely majoritarian Electoral College system, a politician has no choice but to align himself with one of the major parties. Therefore, just like the majority voter blocs observed in other countries, those in the United States are an institutionally driven phenomenon.

Second, even though a majority of voters tend to vote for the same party, they still have salient disagreements on secondary cleavages. Any majority group we observe is simply a large number of disagreeing groups that decide to vote for a common party label for whatever institutional reasons there may be. Their secondary cleavages, such as foreign policy and environmental issues, may have been expressed during primary elections and frequent cross-voting in the legislature.

Dealing with the Problem of Endogenous Democracy

I have restricted the sample to established democracies. However, one could argue that the quality and durability of democracy may be endogenous to the absence of a majority voter bloc. It could be that a country satisfies my sample selection criteria exactly because none of its parties has been dominant.

In order to tackle this problem, I enlarge the sample to check whether marginal democracies (or "open anocracy" according to Marshall, Jaggers, and Gurr 2014) have a different pattern. These countries by definition have irregular electoral cycles and unreliable voting data. But for the purpose of my test, the inaccuracy of these data may not be fatal. The voting records of these countries are most likely biased toward incumbents because they are the ones who are best able to commit electoral fraud. If dominant parties are rare even under these rigged voting data, they would have a harder time surviving under free and fair elections. I also lower the number of election requirements to three in order to include younger and shorter-lived democracies.

Thus, 24 more countries are added to the dataset. Although majority voter blocs do seem more common in these less democratic systems (6 out of 24 countries), we can easily tell that none of these majority parties is a cleavage phenomenon. Table 11 contains an exhaustive list of the six countries with majority voter blocs and their key institutional and electoral data. The top three countries, Nigeria, Georgia, and Senegal, all witnessed power alternation after a few democratic elections, suggesting a lack of unified majority groups.

In the short democratic period of Myanmar, even though the same party, the Anti-Fascist People's Freedom League (AFPFL), stayed in power, it experienced a major split before the third election (Frasch 2001: 598). In fact by the end of the democratic period the party was still searching for an effective label, which resulted in an attempt to institutionalize a state religion and consequent political instability. In addition, the country's electoral system, which allowed a voter to cast multiple votes for multiple seats in the same district, was also notoriously disproportional, which makes any cleavage explanation less likely.

The last two countries, Mozambique and Malaysia, do have highly stable majority parties. Mozambique's FRELIMO (The Mozambique Liberation Front) has survived five elections under a proportional electoral system. Malaysia's National Front has ruled the country since independence and won 13 multiparty elections under a moderately restrictive electoral system (meaning a plurality system with a large assembly size). However, if we consider the third criterion in table 11, we find the dominance of these parties to be questionable. In Mozambique, there does not exist any ethnic, linguistic, or religious group that is nearly as large as 50 percent of the population. Any party that has a chance of winning a majority of popular votes must be a multiethnic and multireligious coalition. Malaysia does have a Malay-Muslim majority, but the governing party takes the form of a combination of many ethnic organizations, including those that represent non-Muslim Indian and Chinese populations. Therefore, it would be hard to argue that the majority voter blocs in these two countries reflect sincere voting decisions. The fact that these multiethnic parties stayed dominant may have resulted from insufficient political competition in these countries, as indicated in their Polity scores.

In order to show the patterns of vote concentration after including marginal democracies, I created the map in figure 11. Obviously, even when including fraudulent elections, the general conclusion that majority groups are rare still holds.

TABLE 11. Short-Lived or Marginal Democracies That Tend to Have Majority Voter Blocs

Country	Average Polity Score	Electoral System	One-Party Dominance	Acriptive Identity for the Dominant Party
Nigeria	5.5	Single-member plurality	No	—
Georgia	5.3	Mixed-member majoritarian	No	—
Senegal	7.3	Mixed-member majoritarian	No	—
Myanmar (1948–60)	8.0	Multi-non-transferable vote	Yes	No
Mozambique	5.0	Closed-list PR	Yes	No
Malaysia	4.8	Plurality	Yes	No

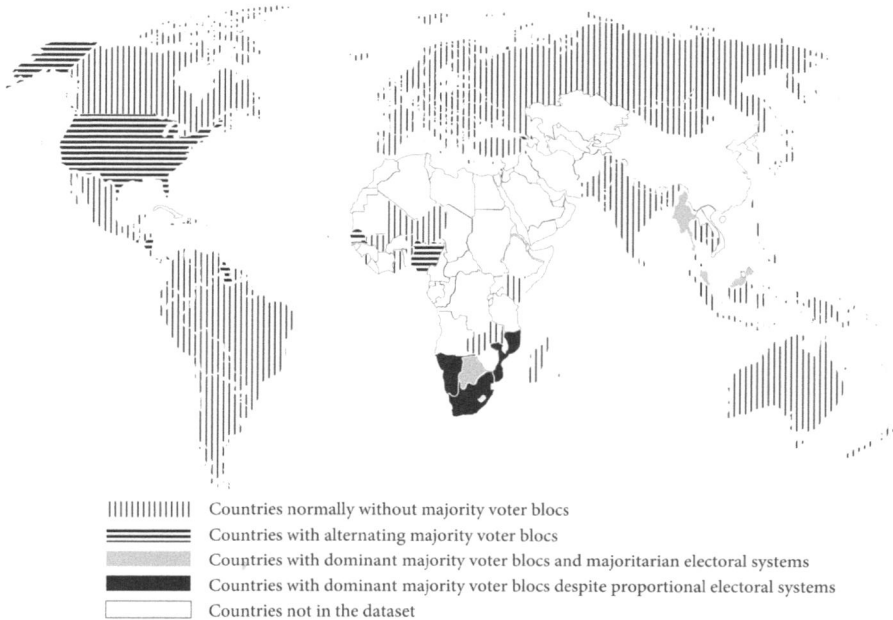

‖‖‖‖‖‖‖‖‖‖	Countries normally without majority voter blocs
▬▬▬▬	Countries with alternating majority voter blocs
(gray)	Countries with dominant majority voter blocs and majoritarian electoral systems
(black)	Countries with dominant majority voter blocs despite proportional electoral systems
(white box)	Countries not in the dataset

Fig. 11. Former and present democracies categorized by vote concentration

The Myth of Unidimensionality and the Case of Northern Ireland

Based on the general cross-national patterns found in this chapter, we can conclude that the unidimensional cleavage structures and consequent stable majorities that concerned many political scientists were actually exceptions in the real world. If a party becomes overly powerful, it almost always has something to do with the restrictiveness of the electoral system or the excessive incumbency advantages that result from a low level of democratic development.

Horowitz (1985) does provide some empirical support for his theory of ethnic party systems. However, the two cases he emphasizes (311–18), Guyana and Trinidad and Tobago, need to be seriously reconsidered in light of the above analyses. Guyana has no majority ethnic group, and therefore the previous dominance of the People's Progressive Party (PPP) more likely resulted from insufficient competition, which is verified by the party's eventual electoral defeat. Trinidad and Tobago has the second-most-restrictive electoral system in the dataset, a plurality formula and an assembly size that ranges from 30 to 41. Even such an institutional environment did not stop the dominant party, the PNM, from losing two elections. Therefore, neither of these party systems really fit the theory of majority group dominance.

I am certainly not arguing that ethnic voting is rare. There is plenty of evidence that supports the importance of ethnic identity in elections (Horowitz 1985; Reilly and Reynolds 1999; Rokkan 1970; Sisk and Reynolds 1998; Chandra, 2007). Instead I argue that ethnic voting by itself is insufficient for the formation of a majority party because of the internal tensions within any majority group. Such parties most often rely on the help of restrictive electoral institutions.

In order to further verify this point, it will be helpful to explore certain within-country variations to see how majority groups respond to institutional changes. However, cases in which a seemingly unidimensional party system actually experienced a major electoral reform that increased proportionality are rare because such reforms hurt the interests of the dominant party. However, there is an imperfect example: the electoral reform of Northern Ireland, a highly autonomous province in the United Kingdom. Exactly because Northern Ireland is not an independent country, its government is subject to pressure from the UK parliament and had to undergo a reform that the original dominant party, the Unionist Party, fiercely opposed.

It is hard to find a party system that is more qualified as unidimensional than Northern Ireland's in the early years after the partition of Ireland. The Catholic and Protestant communities in the province differed not only in their religious beliefs but also over which country they identified with, Ireland or the United Kingdom. These sentiments can be traced back to the prolonged conflict between the British Empire and the Irish nationalists during the better part of the last five centuries, let alone the Great Famine, which killed nearly a quarter of the Irish population under British rule in the mid-nineteenth century. In Miller's (1983) terminology, these distinct issues, which divide the population along the same lines, are called "reinforcing cleavages," the opposite of crosscutting cleavages. Against such a backdrop, the dominance of the Unionist Party, which represented the Protestant majority in the province, mostly descendants of British immigrants, was far from surprising. Can such a system ever experience multipartism? Figure 12 provides a positive answer. In fact, immediately after Northern Ireland changed its plurality system to an STV system, the majority party ceased to exist.

The graph in figure 12 may not be as self-evident as it looks because

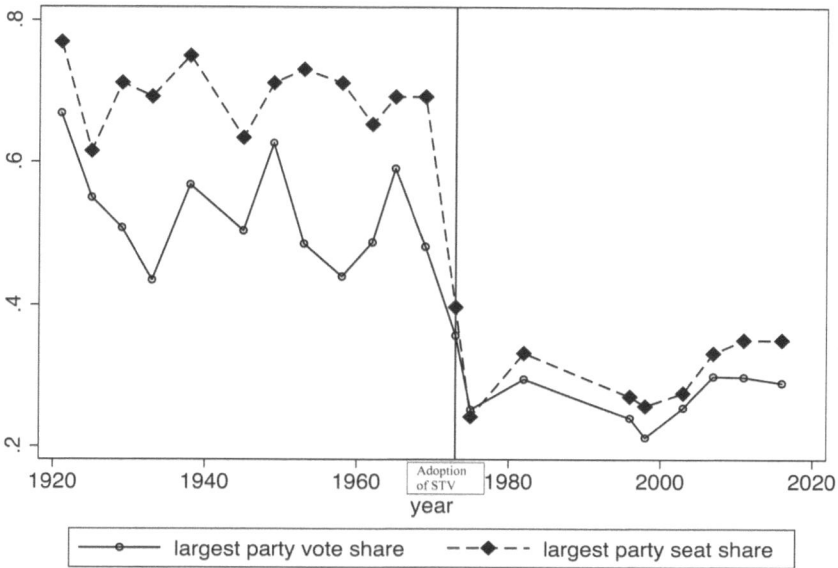

Fig. 12. Evolution of the Northern Ireland party system

of potentially confounding variables. First, the Unionist Party had seen serious internal disagreement even before the electoral reform over the reconciliation policy of the then prime minister, Terence O'Neill. Party members began to run on pro-O'Neill and anti-O'Neill platforms. Was social cleavage evolution happening regardless of the electoral system? The abruptness of the change in party sizes and the sharp contrast between the pre- and postreform periods make it unlikely that this was a cleavage phenomenon.

In fact, internal disagreements within the Protestant community started long before the party system changed. Back in 1956, the most prominent Unionist figure in recent Northern Ireland history, Ian Paisley, had already founded his own alternative Unionist organization, Ulster Protestant Action,[9] arguing that the government had failed to uphold Protestant principles (Smyth 1987: 7). Despite his personal popularity, Paisley's party failed to win any seats in the last election held under the plurality system.

---

9. Ulster Protestant Action later became the Protestant Unionist Party and Democratic Unionist Party, currently the largest party in Northern Ireland.

In other words, the cleavage phenomenon did not make a difference to the party system until electoral restrictiveness was relaxed.

Another problem in figure 12 is that the portrayed elections were not continuous but were interrupted by long periods of direct rule, which was imposed by the British parliament in response to the heightened sectarian conflict. However, the fact that these discontinuous elections picked up the previous level of fragmentation before each interruption exactly shows that party fragmentation in Northern Ireland has an equilibrium range that responds significantly only to electoral systems. The Northern Ireland case is quite effective in illustrating that even the majority group in a seemingly highly unidimensional cleavage structure can be highly fragmented in its policy preferences. Very often it is the restrictive electoral system that magnifies one cleavage at the expense of the others.

In addition to the splitting of large parties, Mitchell (2013) discovered that voters have started transferring their top preferences to candidates from different communities in recent decades,[10] which is a clear sign of social cleavage evolution that points to the decreasing salience of the sectarian divide. This means that while each community was becoming more divided internally the moderate factions in different communities were becoming less divided.

Of course, it is much harder to push the implication to the normative level. After all, the Troubles in Northern Ireland did not quiet down until many decades after the electoral system reform. And many confounding events took place during the period, including direct rule, the implementation of a mandatory cross-community cabinet, and general economic and cultural modernization. It is hard to determine which of these factors assisted, or impeded, the reconciliation process, which is not a question this chapter tries to answer.

Conclusion

The evidence presented here serves to verify the theory proposed in the previous chapter regarding the condition of multipartism: a unidimensional cleavage structure is hard, if not impossible, to sustain unless secondary cleavages are suppressed by the electoral system. This is because a majority group, even a highly salient one, always needs electoral competitiveness to

---

10. The single-transferable-vote system used in Northern Ireland requires voters to rank all the candidates in their respective districts.

hold its representatives accountable and, at the same time, majority politicians must be willing to accommodate the split among the voters in order to increase the job turnover and replace the original leaders. Therefore, most of the majority voter blocs we observe, such as those in the United States, would easily dissolve under a highly proportional system.

Combining this conclusion with the findings in the first half of this book, we can confidently say that under a proportional electoral system, while we cannot exclude the possibility of other problems, at least we do not need to worry much about the tyranny of the majority by the legislative branch. This is because the legislative majority is always fragmented and subject to realignment incentives offered by minorities. Of course, a presidency cannot be proportional by definition, as is repeatedly emphasized by supporters of proportional representation (Lijphart 1999; O'Leary 2013; McGann 2006). Therefore, how friendly the executive branch is to minorities can also be complicated by the existence of an executive presidency. Minorities in a democracy are most protected when the executive branch is controlled by the legislature and the legislature is proportionally elected.

EIGHT

Conclusion

One of my earliest, and probably the discipline's earliest, puzzles regarding democracy is how minorities can survive and thrive under majority rule. We know that it is not a pleasant experience to be on the losing side of the political game in an authoritarian system, but can democracies be more forgiving in that regard? Could it be as hard to live under a tyrannical majority as under a dictator? This project reflects my effort to answer that question.

Inspired by the social choice literature, I started to realize that the most essential defining feature of a democratic system is not so much the size of the winning coalition (as defined in Bueno de Mesquita et al. 2003) but the instability of it. Of course, voting ensures that more people will be on the winning side compared to other decision-making methods. But, more important, it ensures that some portion of that winning side can defect from the rest of the coalition without suffering dire consequences.

Such defections can happen at both the legislative and electorate levels. A legislator can find different allies from bill to bill. A voter can also vote for different parties from election to election. Either way, the end result is that the electoral losers in one bill or election often end up on the winning side in the next one as long as they can find enough defectors. And that is exactly the reason why the dreadful "tyranny of the majority" is rare and, when observed, not as appalling and persistent as the tyranny in countries without regular winner alternation. The more a group feels hurt by a current policy, the more it is willing to offer concessions to other groups to form an alternative winning coalition.

We can easily observe such coalition dynamics in the anti-Trump marches that swept the country in early 2017. It may not be obvious why feminists held signs with women in hijabs or why trade activists stood side by side with environmentalists. It is certainly wrong to say that these groups share a lot of agreement. But democracy makes it possible for them to form an ad hoc coalition in an effort to undermine the current winning coalition in the Electoral College.

Of course, not all democracies are equally friendly to people who change sides. In cases in which a unified party controls the majority of the legislature, those who defect from the majority may risk losing their party support or even their party membership, the most valuable label in political campaigns. In countries with a strong presidency, realignment at the legislative level may not make much difference because the president by himself can decide which laws to enforce. In that case, electoral losers have to depend on realignment at the electorate level to unseat the president, just as in the recent marches, which is certainly much harder than legislative realignment accomplished through a few closed-door meetings. These variations will certainly affect the distributive equality between winners and losers.

How well a country treats the electoral losers, however, is hard to measure empirically. We cannot simply attribute all the inequality in a country to the bias of the government. Lijphart (1999) has some innovative proxies for a "kinder and gentler" democracy, such as a welfare state, environment protection, and the incarceration rate. However, these measures still suffer the lack of normative certainty. So the first task of this book was to find a way to explain and test a minority's bargaining power in a less controversial way. Following the social choice literature, I constructed a hypothetical scenario in which an extremely small democracy, namely, a three-player committee, divided a certain prize. This way the interests of minorities in these minidemocracies can be easily measured by means of the smallest share of accumulated prizes among the three players.

In order to capture the institutional variable that makes the difference, I developed a novel concept I call the "defection cost." It refers to the amount of benefit a player has to give up if he defects from the winning coalition. It is not hard to see that, as theorized in chapter 3 using the three-player game, higher defection costs make it harder for the current electoral losers to induce cycling and reverse their bad luck. In an online bargaining experiment that targets the theory, it is observed that losers under high defection costs catch up with the winners much more slowly.

If the experiment itself was too abstract to convince readers, the series of cross-national analyses I reviewed basically confirmed the same pattern. With different measurements and empirical methods, all the existing large-N studies, regardless of their choice of sample and measurement, agree that countries with multiparty coalition governments (including minority governments that rely on the confidence of more than one party) are associated with more equal distributive outcomes and better minority conditions. It is hard to deny that the instability of the winning coalition does play a major role.

These analyses confirm that Miller (1983) and McGann (2006) are right in concluding that cycling is not as bad as early social choice theorists suggested it is. It does not make democracy "meaningless"; on the contrary, it is the most important reason that most democratic systems are so friendly toward their political losers. If one has the freedom to choose a country in which to live, all else held constant, he should try to find a country without a stable winning coalition. And if a political scientist is commissioned to design a political institution, he should ensure that the defection costs for the winning coalition members are not high enough to impede frequent cycling.

As the institutional design proceeds, another question necessarily emerges. Is there really an institutional feature that can ensure a low defection cost? If a group is so unified that any defector is considered a traitor and immediately despised by his group members, will any institution make a difference? In other words, if defection cost is just a social cleavage phenomenon, what can we do about it?

Fortunately, it is not. I used the last two chapters to show that a unified majority group is next to impossible. Why do we observe so much seemingly unidimensional political competition? In most of the cases, it is no more than an institutional phenomenon. Small parties either fail to gain representation because of the Duvergerian mechanical effect or fail to win votes because of the Duvergerian psychological effects. I used an exhaustive approach for the countries that normally have a majority voting bloc thanks to the small number of them. I show that with merely two exceptions these countries are characterized by either a large number of swing voters, such as in the United States, or an extremely restrictive electoral system, such as in Botswana and Trinidad and Tobago. It can be predicted that their majority parties will not survive a highly proportional electoral system.

James Madison (2003 [1787]: 78) argued in Federalist 10 that "the smaller the society . . . the more frequently a majority will be found in the same party," which is why he argued for a large "republic." But keep in mind that in Madison's time the total population of the American colonies was less than three million (US Department of Commerce 1975: 1168). So the large republic he craved was really a small agrarian nation by today's standards. The complexity of modern societies means that there is little chance for a majority of voters to share the same salient identity. In the short run, they may be united by the same issue. But their allegiance will eventually be tested by the numerous issues on which they disagree. Instead of trying to unify the voters in any way, the most important job of institutional designers is to encourage the members of any potential majority group to politically express their internal disagreements, which is the ultimate guard against the tyranny of the majority.

These findings have strong implications for current US politics. The defection costs embedded in American institutions were high to start with because of a powerful executive presidency. The losers in a presidential election always have a hard time promoting their agendas because the president alone has the power to veto legislation and selectively enforce the law. Moreover, the legislative realignment is irrelevant to presidential survival. However, the recent party polarization and presidentialization make even congressional politics revolve more exclusively around the presidency, and therefore even defection from the winning legislative coalition becomes less likely. Under a system like this, the country has to count on electing a moderate president, which has become less and less likely in a polarized two-party system.

Of course, reforming American institutions in the direction of higher proportionality and a weaker presidency is a daunting task. Neither of the two large parties will be interested in giving up part of its power to small parties that may emerge from such reforms. This is exactly why it is so important to make such knowledge available to the general public and rely on voters to reward politicians who have the courage to initiate meaningful reforms. I wish I could have written this book in a more accessible style, but as a nonnative English speaker, I think I must leave that job to more capable hands.

Finally, with the findings of this book, I will be much better equipped in my debate with the democracy skeptics back in China. They have been constantly asking tough questions that I do not know how to answer. What if the Uighurs begin to drive Han Chinese away from Xinjiang when they are given the right to vote? What if Chinese nationalists wage a war against minorities that seek independence? What if organized poor migrants hit back at discriminating locals and overdo it? Everyone knows that democracy is statistically beneficial, but what if a country is too divided to enjoy its benefits? Right now, I can simply tell them that there is a way to divide those formidable majorities and restrain their behavior. Democracy in general may not be sufficiently reliable, but a democratic system with high proportionality and a parliamentary executive in which political power can cycle across different winning coalitions is a fairly promising institutional choice. Such confidence is extremely important because, as Lijphart (1977: 3) wisely warns, "If politicians and political scientists are convinced that democracy cannot work in the plural societies of the Third World, they will not even try to introduce it or to make it work."

References

Abney, Ronni, James Adams, Michael Clark, Malcolm Easton, Lawrence Ezrow, Spyros Kosmidis, and Anja Neundorf. 2013. "When does valence matter? Heightened valence effects for governing parties during election campaigns." *Party Politics* 19.1: 61–82.

Adams, James F., Samuel Merrill III, and Bernard Grofman. 2005. *A unified theory of party competition: A cross-national analysis integrating spatial and behavioral factors.* Cambridge University Press.

Adamson, Fiona B. 2001. "Democratization and the domestic sources of foreign policy: Turkey in the 1974 Cyprus crisis." *Political Science Quarterly* 116.2: 277–303.

Almond, Gabriel A. 1956. "Comparative political systems." *Journal of Politics* 18.3: 391–409.

Amorim Neto, Octavio, and Gary W. Cox. 1997. "Electoral institutions, cleavage structures, and the number of parties." *American Journal of Political Science* 41.1: 149–74.

Armingeon, Klaus. 2002. "The effects of negotiation democracy: A comparative analysis." *European Journal of Political Research* 41.1: 81–105.

Arrow, Kenneth J. 2012. *Social choice and individual values.* 3rd ed. Yale University Press. Originally published in 1951.

Banks, Jeffrey S., and Farid Gasmi. 1987. "Endogenous agenda formation in three-person committees." *Social Choice and Welfare* 4.2: 133–52.

Baron, David P., and John A. Ferejohn. 1989. "Bargaining in legislatures." *American Political Science Review* 83.4: 1181–1206.

Barry, Brian. 2002. *Culture and equality: An egalitarian critique of multiculturalism.* Harvard University Press.

Battaglini, Marco, and Thomas R. Palfrey. 2012. "The dynamics of distributive politics." *Economic Theory* 49.3: 739–77.

Benabou, Roland. 2000. "Unequal societies: Income distribution and the social contract." *American Economic Review* 90.1: 96–129.

Benedetto, Giacomo, and Simon Hix. 2007. "The rejected, the ejected, and the dejected: Explaining government rebels in the 2001–2005 British House of Commons." *Comparative Political Studies* 40.7: 755–81.

Black, Duncan. 1948. "On the rationale of group decision-making." *Journal of Political Economy* 56.1: 23–34.

Bloomberg, Michael R. 2016. "The risk I will not take." Bloomberg, March 7. https://www.bloomberg.com/opinion/articles/2016-03-07/the-2016-election-risk-that-michael-bloomberg-won-t-take

Boix, Carles. 1999. "Setting the rules of the game: The choice of electoral systems in advanced democracies." *American Political Science Review* 93.3: 609–24.

Bollard, Alan. 1994. "New Zealand." In J. Williamson, ed., *The political economy of policy reform*. Peterson Institute.

Bond, Patrick. 2014. *Elite transition: From apartheid to neoliberalism in South Africa*. Pluto Press.

Bormann, Nils-Christian, and Matt Golder. 2013. "Democratic electoral systems around the world, 1946–2011." *Electoral Studies* 32.2: 360–69.

Bowler, Shaun, David M. Farrell, and Robin T. Pettitt. 2005. "Expert opinion on electoral systems: So which electoral system is 'best'?" *Journal of Elections, Public Opinion, and Parties* 15.1: 3–19.

Bowler, Shaun, Bernard Grofman, and André Blais. 2009. "The United States: A case of Duvergerian equilibrium." In Shaun Bowler, Bernard Grofman, and André Blais, eds., *Duverger's Law of Plurality Voting*. Springer New York. 135–46.

Bryan, Dominic. 2000. *Orange parades: The politics of ritual, tradition, and control*. Pluto Press.

Buchanan, James M., and Gordon Tullock. 1999. *The calculus of consent: Logical foundations of constitutional democracy*. Liberty Fund.

Bueno de Mesquita, Bruce, Alastair Smith, Randolph M. Siverson, and James D. Morrow. 2003. *The logic of political survival*. MIT Press.

Bureau of Democracy, Human Rights, and Labor. 2014. "2013 Human Rights Reports: Ethiopia." http://www.state.gov/j/drl/rls/hrrpt/2013/af/220113.htm

Butenschøn, Nils A. 1985. "Conflict management in plural societies: The consociational democracy formula." *Scandinavian Political Studies* 8.1–2: 85–103.

Butler, Anthony. 2009. *Contemporary South Africa*. Palgrave Macmillan.

Buttice, Matthew K., and Walter J. Stone. 2012. "Candidates matter: Policy and quality differences in congressional elections." *Journal of Politics* 74.3: 870–87.

Cain, Bruce, John Ferejohn, and Morris Fiorina. 1987. *The personal vote: Constituency service and electoral independence*. Harvard University Press.

Camerer, Colin. 2003. *Behavioral game theory: Experiments in strategic interaction*. Princeton University Press.

Caramani, Daniele. 2004. *The nationalization of politics: The formation of national electorates and party systems in Western Europe*. Cambridge University Press.

Carey, John M. 2009. *Legislative voting and accountability*. Cambridge University Press.

Carey, John M., and Simon Hix. 2011. "The electoral sweet spot: Low-magnitude proportional electoral systems." *American Journal of Political Science* 55.2: 383–97.

Carey, John M., and Matthew Soberg Shugart. 1995. "Incentives to cultivate a personal vote: A rank ordering of electoral formulas." *Electoral Studies* 14.4: 417–39.

Carr, Adam. N.d. *Psephos: Adam Carr's election archive*. http://psephos.adam-carr.net

Chand, Satish. 1997. "Ethnic conflict, income inequity, and growth in independent Fiji." Australian National University Digital Collections Library. http://hdl.handle.net/1885/40388

Chandra, Kanchan. 2005. "Ethnic parties and democratic stability." *Perspectives on Politics* 3.2: 235–52.

Chandra, Kanchan. 2007. *Why ethnic parties succeed: Patronage and ethnic head counts in India*. Cambridge University Press.

Cheibub, José Antonio. 2007. *Presidentialism, parliamentarism, and democracy*. Cambridge University Press.

Cheibub, José Antonio, Adam Przeworski, Fernando Papaterra Limongi Neto, and Michael M. Alvarez. 1996. "What makes democracies endure?" *Journal of Democracy* 7.1: 39–55.

Clark, William R., and Matt Golder. 2006. "Rehabilitating Duverger's theory testing the mechanical and strategic modifying effects of electoral laws." *Comparative Political Studies* 39.6: 679–708.

Cox, Gary W. 1987. *The efficient secret: The cabinet and the development of political parties in Victorian England*. Cambridge University Press.

Cox, Gary W. 1997. *Making votes count: Strategic coordination in the world's electoral systems*. Cambridge University Press.

Cox, Gary W., and Mathew D. McCubbins. 1986. "Electoral politics as a redistributive game." *Journal of Politics* 48.2: 370–89.

Crouch, Harold. 2001. "Managing ethnic tensions through affirmative action: The Malaysian experience." In Nat J. Colletta, Teck Ghee Lim, and Anita Kelles-Viitanen, eds., *Social cohesion and conflict prevention in Asia: Managing diversity through development*. World Bank. 225–62.

Cunningham, Michael. 2001. *British government policy in Northern Ireland, 1969–2000*. Manchester University Press.

Cunningham, William H., W. Thomas Anderson, and John H. Murphy. 1974. "Are students real people?" *Journal of Business* 47:399–409.

Dahl, Robert A. 2013. *A preface to democratic theory*. University of Chicago Press.

Downs, Anthony. 1957. "An economic theory of political action in a democracy." *Journal of Political Economy* 65.2: 135–50.

Duverger, Maurice. 1959. *Political parties: Their organization and activity in the modern state*. Translated by Barbara North and Robert North. Methuen. Originally published in 1951.

Eller, Jack David, and Reed M. Coughlan. 1993. "The poverty of primordialism: The demystification of ethnic attachments." *Ethnic and Racial Studies* 16.2: 183–202.

Enis, Ben M., Keith K. Cox, and James E. Stafford. 1972. "Students as subjects in consumer behavior experiments." *Journal of Marketing Research* 9.1: 72–74.

Epstein, David. 1997. "Uncovering some subtleties of the uncovered set: Social choice theory and distributive politics." *Social Choice and Welfare* 15.1: 81–93.

Fearon, James D. 1998. "Commitment problems and the spread of ethnic conflict." In David A. Lake and Donald S. Rothchild, eds., *The international spread of ethnic conflict*. Princeton University Press. 107–26.

Fearon, James D. 2003. "Ethnic and cultural diversity by country." *Journal of Economic Growth* 8.2: 195–222.

Fearon, James D., and David D. Laitin. 2003. "Ethnicity, insurgency, and civil war." *American Political Science Review* 97.1: 75–90.

Ferejohn, John, Morris Fiorina, and Richard D. McKelvey. 1987. "Sophisticated voting and agenda independence in the distributive politics setting." *American Journal of Political Science* 31.1: 169–193.

Ferree, Karen E. 2010. *Framing the race in South Africa: The political origins of racial census elections.* Cambridge University Press.

Ferree, Karen E., G. Bingham Powell, and Ethan Scheiner. 2014. "Context, electoral rules, and party systems." *Annual Review of Political Science* 17:421–39.

Fiorina, Morris P., Samuel J. Abrams, and Jeremy Pope. 2005. *Culture war? The myth of a polarized America.* Pearson Longman.

Frasch, Tilman. 2001. "Myanmar (Burma)." In Dieter Nohlen, Florian Grotz, and Christof Hartmann, *Elections in Asia: A data handbook.* Vol. 1. Oxford University Press. 597–620.

Fréchette, Guillaume R., John H. Kagel, and Massimo Morelli. 2005. "Gamson's Law versus non-cooperative bargaining theory." *Games and Economic Behavior* 51.2: 365–90.

Freedom House. 2015. "Methodology." Freedom House. https://www.freedom house.org/report/freedom-world-2015/methodology#.VZ_3X2CTk6V

Friedman, Daniel, and Shyam Sunder. 1994. *Experimental methods: A primer for economists.* Cambridge University Press.

Friedman, Milton. 1962. *Capitalism and freedom.* University of Chicago Press.

Gallagher, Michael. 1988. "Ireland: The increasing role of the centre." In Michael Gallagher and Michael Marsh, eds., *Candidate selection in comparative perspective: The secret garden of politics.* Sage Publications. 119–44.

Garman, Christopher, Stephan Haggard, and Eliza J. Willis. 2001. "Fiscal decentralization: A political theory with Latin American cases." *World Politics* 53.2: 205–36.

Gerring, John, and Strom C. Thacker. 2008. *A centripetal theory of democratic governance.* Cambridge University Press.

Good, Irving John. 1971. "A note on Condorcet sets." *Public Choice* 10.1: 97–101.

Grim, Brian J. 2012. "Religion, law, and social conflict in the twenty-first century: Findings from sociological research." *Oxford Journal of Law and Religion* 1.1: 249–71.

Grumm, John G. 1958. "Theories of electoral systems." *Midwest Journal of Political Science* 2.4: 357–76.

Güth, Werner, and Reinhard Tietz. 1990. "Ultimatum bargaining behavior: A survey and comparison of experimental results." *Journal of Economic Psychology* 11.3: 417–49.

Haque, M. Shamsul. 2003. "The role of the state in managing ethnic tensions in Malaysia: A critical discourse." *American Behavioral Scientist* 47.3: 240–66.

Hasan, Mushirul. 2002. "The BJP's intellectual agenda: Textbooks and imagined history." *South Asia: Journal of South Asian Studies* 25.3: 187–209.

Hazan, Reuven Y., and Gideon Rahat. 2010. *Democracy within parties: Candidate selection methods and their political consequences.* Oxford University Press.

Holt, Charles A., and Susan K. Laury. 2002. "Risk aversion and incentive effects." *American Economic Review* 92.5: 1644–55.

Horowitz, Donald L. 1985. *Ethnic groups in conflict*. University of California Press.

Horowitz, Donald L. 1991. *A democratic South Africa? Constitutional engineering in a divided society*. University of California Press.

Horowitz, Donald L. 2002. "Constitutional design: Proposals versus processes." In Andrew Reynolds, ed., *The architecture of democracy*. Oxford University Press. 15–36.

Inglehart, Ronald. 1977. *The silent revolution: Changing values and political styles among western publics*. Princeton University Press.

Irwin, Colin. 1991. *Education and the development of social integration in divided societies*. Northern Ireland Council for Integrated Education.

Iversen, Torben, and David Soskice. 2006. "Electoral institutions and the politics of coalitions: Why some democracies redistribute more than others." *American Political Science Review* 100.2: 165–81.

Jacobson, Gary C. 2013. *The politics of congressional elections*. 8th ed. HarperCollins.

Jarman, Neil. 2003. "From outrage to apathy? The disputes over parades, 1995–2003." *Global Review of Ethnopolitics* 3.1: 92–105.

Johnson, Eric J., Colin Camerer, Sankar Sen, and Talia Rymon. 2002. "Detecting failures of backward induction: Monitoring information search in sequential bargaining." *Journal of Economic Theory* 104.1: 16–47.

Kalandrakis, Anastassios. 2004. "A three-player dynamic majoritarian bargaining game." *Journal of Economic Theory* 116.2: 294–14.

Kam, Christopher J. 2009. *Party discipline and parliamentary politics*. Cambridge University Press.

Kiewiet, D. Roderick, and Mathew D. McCubbins. 1991. *The logic of delegation*. University of Chicago Press.

Krauss, Ellis S., and Robert J. Pekkanen. 2011. *The rise and fall of Japan's LDP: Political party organizations as historical institutions*. Cornell University Press.

Kumar, Krishna. 1990. "Hindu revivalism and education in north-central India." *Social Scientist* 18.10: 4–26.

Lee, Aaron Ken. 2015. *China's economy, the hidden truths: China's economy seen in the undercurrent of organized unaccountability*. Global Era Public Interest Info Network.

Lewin, Leif, Barbro Lewin, Hanna Bäck, and Lina Westin. 2008. "A kinder, gentler democracy? The consensus model and Swedish disability politics." *Scandinavian Political Studies* 31.3: 291–310.

Li, Yuhui. 2018. "Electoral system effects re-examined using the largest vote share variable." *Democratization* 25.1: 58–77.

Li, Yuhui, and Matthew S. Shugart. 2016. "The Seat Product Model of the effective number of parties: A case for applied political science." *Electoral Studies* 41:23–34.

Lijphart, Arend. 1969. "Consociational democracy." *World Politics* 21.2: 207–25.

Lijphart, Arend. 1975. *The politics of accommodation: Pluralism and democracy in the Netherlands*. University of California Press.

Lijphart, Arend. 1977. *Democracy in plural societies: A comparative exploration*. Yale University Press.

Lijphart, Arend. 1985. *Power-sharing in South Africa*. Institute of International Studies, University of California.

Lijphart, Arend. 1991. "Constitutional choices for new democracies." *Journal of Democracy* 2.1: 72–84.

Lijphart, Arend. 1995. "Self-determination versus pre-determination of ethnic minorities in power-sharing systems." In Will Kymlicka. ed., *The rights of minority cultures*. Oxford University Press.

Lijphart, Arend. 1999. *Patterns of democracy: Government forms and performance in thirty-six democracies*. Yale University Press.

Lijphart, Arend. 2002. "The wave of power-sharing democracy." In Andrew Reynolds, ed., *The architecture of democracy*. Oxford University Press. 37–54.

Lijphart, Arend. 2004. "Constitutional design for divided societies." *Journal of Democracy* 15.2: 96–109.

Linz, Juan J. 1990a. "The perils of presidentialism." *Journal of Democracy* 1 (Winter): 51–69.

Linz, Juan J. 1990b. "The virtues of parliamentarism." *Journal of Democracy* 1 (Fall): 84–91.

Linz, Juan J., and Alfred C. Stepan. eds. 1978. *The Breakdown of democratic regimes: Crisis, breakdown and reequilibration*. Johns Hopkins University Press.

Lipset, Seymour Martin. 1981. *Political man*. Expanded ed. Johns Hopkins University Press. Originally published in 1960.

Lipset, Seymour Martin, and Stein Rokkan. 1967. "Cleavage structures, party systems, and voter alignments: An introduction." In Seymour Martin Lipset and Stein Rokkan, eds., *Party systems and voter alignments: Cross-national perspectives*. Free Press. 1–64.

Loewenstein, George F., Leigh Thompson, and Max H. Bazerman. 1989. "Social utility and decision making in interpersonal contexts." *Journal of Personality and Social Psychology* 57.3: 426–41.

Lovestone, Jay. 1928. "The Sixth World Congress of the Communist International." *Communist* 7.11: 659–75.

Lupia, Arthur, and Kaare Strøm. 1995. "Coalition termination and the strategic timing of parliamentary elections." *American Political Science Review* 89.3: 648–65.

Macias, Amanda, and Mike Nudelman. 2015. "Here are the salaries of 13 major world leaders." *Business Insider*, March 19. http://www.businessinsider.com/salaries-of-13-major-world-leaders-2015-3

Mackie, Gerry. 2003. *Democracy defended*. Cambridge University Press.

Madison, James. 2003. "Federalist 10." In Clinton Rossiter, ed., *The Federalist Papers*. Penguin Group. Originally published in 1787.

Maeda, Ko. 2010. "Two modes of democratic breakdown: A competing risks analysis of democratic durability." *Journal of Politics* 72.4: 1129–43.

Magaloni, Beatriz. 2006. *Voting for autocracy: Hegemonic party survival and its demise in Mexico*. Cambridge University Press.

Mainwaring, Scott, and Aníbal Pérez Liñán. 1997. "Party discipline in the Brazilian constitutional congress." *Legislative Studies Quarterly* 22.4: 453–83.

Mainwaring, Scott, and Matthew Shugart. 1994. "Juan Linz, presidentialism, and democracy." In Scott Mainwaring and Arturo Valenzuela, eds., *Politics, society, and democracy, Latin America: Essays in Honor of Juan Linz*. Westview. 141–70.

Marshall, Alfred. 1920. *Principles of Economics*, revised ed. Macmillan; reprinted by Prometheus Books.

Marshall, Monty G., Keith Jaggers, and Ted Robert Gurr. 2014. *Polity IV project*. Center for International Development and Conflict Management, University of Maryland, College Park.

Mayhew, David R. 1974. *Congress: The electoral connection*. Yale University Press.

McClenahan, Carol, Ed Cairns, Seamus Dunn, and Valerie Morgan. 1996. "Intergroup friendships: Integrated and desegregated schools in Northern Ireland." *Journal of Social Psychology* 136.5: 549–58.

McGann, Anthony. 2006. *The logic of democracy: Reconciling equality, deliberation, and minority protection*. University of Michigan Press.

McGarry, John, and Brendan O'Leary. 2004. "Introduction: Consociational theory and Northern Ireland." In John McGarry and Brendan O'Leary, eds. *The Northern Ireland conflict: Consociational engagements*. Oxford University Press. 1–61.

McGarry, John, and Brendan O'Leary. 2006a. "Consociational theory, Northern Ireland's conflict, and its agreement, part 2: What critics of consociation can learn from Northern Ireland." *Government and Opposition* 41.2: 249–77.

McGarry, John, and Brendan O'Leary. 2006b. "Consociational theory, Northern Ireland's conflict, and its agreement, part 1: What consociationalists can learn from Northern Ireland." *Government and Opposition* 41.1: 43–63.

McGarry, John, and Brendan O'Leary. 2009. "Power shared after the deaths of thousands." In Rupert Taylor, ed., *Consociational theory: McGarry and O'Leary and the Northern Ireland conflict*. Routledge. 15–84.

Mershon, Carol. 1999. "The costs of coalition: A five-nation comparison." In Shaun Bowler, David Farrell, and Richard Katz, eds., *Party discipline and parliamentary government*. Ohio State University Press. 227–65.

Mershon, Carol, and Olga Shvetsova. 2013. "The microfoundations of party system stability in legislatures." *Journal of Politics* 75.4: 865–78.

Mill, John Stuart. 2002. *On liberty*. Dover. Originally published in 1859.

Miller, David. 1995. *On nationality*. Oxford University Press.

Miller, Nicholas R. 1980. "A new solution set for tournaments and majority voting: Further graph-theoretical approaches to the theory of voting." *American Journal of Political Science* 24.1: 68–96.

Miller, Nicholas R. 1983. "Pluralism and social choice." *American Political Science Review* 77.3: 734–47.

Minorities at Risk Project. 2009. "Minorities at Risk Dataset."Center for International Development and Conflict Management, University of Maryland, College Park. http://www.mar.umd.edu/mar_data.asp (retrieved on 07/10/2015).

Mitchell, Paul. 2014. "The single transferable vote and ethnic conflict: The evidence from Northern Ireland." *Electoral Studies* 33:246–57.

Morelli, Massimo. 1999. "Demand competition and policy compromise in legislative bargaining." *American Political Science Review* 93.4: 809–20.

Morgan, Valerie, Grace Fraser, Seamus Dunn, and Ed Cairns. 1992. "Views from outside: Other professionals' views of the religiously integrated schools in Northern Ireland." *British Journal of Religious Education* 14.3: 169–77.

Moser, Robert G., and Ethan Scheiner. 2012. *Electoral systems and political context:*

How the effects of rules vary across new and established democracies. Cambridge University Press.

Nagel, Jack H. 1994. "What political scientists can learn from the 1993 electoral reform in New Zealand." *PS: Political Science and Politics.* 27.3: 525–29.

Nohlen, Dieter. 2005. *Elections in the Americas: A data handbook.* Oxford University Press.

Nohlen, Dieter, Florian Grotz, and Christof Hartmann. 2001. *Elections in Asia: A data handbook.* Oxford University Press.

Nohlen, Dieter, Michael Krennerich, and Bernhard Thibaut. 1999. *Elections in Africa: A data handbook.* Oxford University Press.

Nohlen, Dieter, and Philip Stover. 2010. *Elections in Europe: A data handbook.* Nomos Verlagsgesellschaft.

Norris, Pippa. 2008. *Driving democracy: Do power-sharing institutions work?* Cambridge University Press.

Norris, Pippa. 2012. *Making democratic governance work: How regimes shape prosperity, welfare, and peace.* Cambridge University Press.

O'Leary Brendan. 2004. "The Anglo-Irish Agreement: Folly or statecraft?" In John McGarry and Brendan O'Leary, eds. *The Northern Ireland conflict: Consociational engagements.* Oxford University Press. 62–96.

O'Leary, Brendan. 2013. "Power sharing in deeply divided places: An advocate's introduction." In Joanne McEvoy and Brendan O'Leary, eds., *Power sharing in deeply divided places.* University of Pennsylvania Press. 1–66.

Okun, Arthur M. 1977. *Equality and efficiency: The big tradeoff.* Brookings Institution.

Onishi, Norimitsu, and Selam Gebrekidan. 2018. "Hit men and power: South Africa's leaders are killing one another." *New York Times,* September 30.

Ordeshook, Peter C., and Olga V. Shvetsova. 1994. "Ethnic heterogeneity, district magnitude, and the number of parties." *American Journal of Political Science* 38.1: 100–123.

Persson, Torsten, and Guido Tabellini. 2003. *The economic effects of constitutions.* MIT Press.

Pigou, Arthur Cecil. 1932. *The economics of welfare.* 4th ed. Macmillan. Originally published in 1920.

Popkin, Samuel L. 1994. *The reasoning voter: Communication and persuasion in presidential campaigns.* University of Chicago Press.

Powell, G. Bingham. 2000. *Elections as instruments of democracy: Majoritarian and proportional visions.* Yale University Press.

Preisvergleich.de. 2013. "Salary Atlas of the 27 EU countries." http://www.preis vergleich.de/presse/customs/uploads/2013/05/PVG_Pressemappe_Abgeord neten-Gehälter_EN.pdf

Przeworski, Adam, Micharel E. Alvarez, Jose Antonia Cheibub, and Fernando Limongi. 2000. *Democracy and development: Political institutions and well-being in the world, 1950–1990.* Cambridge University Press.

Rabin, Matthew. 1993. "Incorporating fairness into game theory and economics." *American Economic Review* 83.5: 1281–1302.

Rabushka, Alvin, and Kenneth A. Shepsle. 1972. *Politics in plural societies.* Stanford University Press.

Rae, Douglas W. 1967. *The political consequences of electoral laws.* Yale University Press.

Rae, Douglas W., and Michael Taylor. 1970. *The analysis of political cleavages.* Yale University Press.

Reilly, Benjamin. 2001. *Democracy in divided societies: Electoral engineering for conflict management.* Cambridge University Press.

Reilly, Benjamin. 2002. "Electoral systems for divided societies." *Journal of Democracy* 13.2: 156–70.

Reilly, Benjamin. 2004. *Elections in post-conflict societies.* United Nations University Press.

Reilly, Benjamin. 2006. "Political engineering and party politics in conflict-prone societies." *Democratization* 13.5: 811–27.

Reilly, Benjamin, and Andrew Reynolds. 1999. *Electoral systems and conflict in divided societies.* National Academies Press.

Reynolds, Andrew. 1995. "The Case for Proportionality." *Journal of Democracy* 6.4: 117–24.

Riker, William H. 1962. *The theory of political coalitions.* Yale University Press.

Riker, William H. 1982. *Liberalism against populism: A confrontation between the theory of democracy and the theory of social choice.* Waveland Press.

Riker, William H., and Peter C. Ordeshook. 1973. *An introduction to positive political theory.* Prentice Hall.

Robbers, Gerhard. ed. 2007. *Encyclopedia of world constitutions.* Facts on File.

Roeder, Philip G. 1993. *Red sunset: The failure of Soviet politics.* Princeton University Press.

Rokkan, Stein. 1970. "Nation-building, cleavage formation, and the structuring of mass politics." In *Citizens, elections, parties: Approaches to the comparative study of the processes of development.* ECPR Press. 72–144.

Ross, Dorothy. 1992. *The origins of American social science.* Cambridge University Press.

Ross, Marc Howard. 2001. "Psychocultural interpretations and dramas: Identity dynamics in ethnic conflict." *Political Psychology* 22.1: 157–78.

Rothchild, Donald, and Philip G. Roeder. 2005. "Power sharing as an impediment to peace and democracy." In Philip G. Roeder and Donald Rothchild, eds., *Sustainable peace: Power and democracy after civil wars.* Cornell University Press. 29–50.

Samuels, David J., and Matthew S. Shugart. 2010. *Presidents, parties, and prime ministers: How the separation of powers affects party organization and behavior.* Cambridge University Press.

Shugart, Matthew S. 1995. "The electoral cycle and institutional sources of divided presidential government." *American Political Science Review* 89.2: 327–43.

Shugart, Matthew S. 1999. "Presidentialism, parliamentarism, and the provision of collective goods in less-developed countries." *Constitutional Political Economy* 10.1: 53–88.

Shugart, Matthew S. 2005. "Semi-presidential systems: Dual executive and mixed authority patterns." *French Politics* 3.3: 323–51.

Shugart, Matthew S., and John M. Carey. 1992. *Presidents and assemblies: Constitutional design and electoral dynamics.* Cambridge University Press.

Shugart, Matthew S., and Rein Taagepera. 2017. *Votes from seats: Logical models of electoral systems.* Cambridge University Press.

Shugart, Matthew S., and Martin P. Wattenberg, eds. 2001. *Mixed-member electoral systems: The best of both worlds?* Oxford University Press.

Singer, Matthew S., and Laura B. Stephenson. 2009. "The political context and Duverger's theory: Evidence at the district level." *Electoral Studies* 28.3: 480–91.

Sisk, Timothy D., and Andrew Reynolds. 1998. *Elections and conflict management in Africa.* US Institute of Peace Press.

Smith, Adam. 1977. *An inquiry into the nature and causes of the wealth of nations.* University of Chicago Press. Originally published in 1776.

Smith, Vernon L., and James M. Walker. 1993. "Monetary rewards and decision cost in experimental economics." *Economic Inquiry* 31.2: 245–61.

Smyth, Clifford. 1987. *Ian Paisley: Voice of Protestant Ulster.* Scottish Academic Press.

Sriskandarajah, Dhananjayan. 2005. "Socio-economic inequality and ethno-political conflict: Some observations from Sri Lanka." *Contemporary South Asia* 14.3: 341–56.

Stokes, Donald E. 1963. "Spatial models of party competition." *American Political Science Review* 57.2: 368–77.

Stokes, Donald E. 1992. "Valence politics." In Dennis Kavanagh, ed., *Electoral politics.* Clarendon. 141–64.

Stoll, Heather. 2008. "Social cleavages and the number of parties: How the measures you choose affect the answers you get." *Comparative Political Studies* 41.11: 1439–65.

Stoll, Heather. 2013. *Changing societies, changing party systems.* Cambridge University Press.

Stone, Walter J., and Elizabeth N. Simas. 2010. "Candidate valence and ideological positions in US House elections." *American Journal of Political Science* 54.2: 371–88.

Struthers, Cory L., Yuhui Li, and Matthew S. Shugart. 2018. "Introducing new multilevel datasets: Party systems at the district and national levels." *Research and Politics* 5.4: 1–4.

Sundar, Nandini. 2005. "Teaching to hate: The Hindu right's pedagogical program." In E. Thomas Ewing, ed., *Revolution and pedagogy.* Palgrave Macmillan US. 195–218.

Svolik, Milan W. 2008. "Authoritarian reversals and democratic consolidation." *American Political Science Review* 102.2: 153–68.

Svolik, Milan W. 2015. "Which democracies will last? Coups, incumbent takeovers, and the dynamic of democratic consolidation." *British Journal of Political Science* 45.4: 715–38.

Taagepera, Rein. 2007. *Predicting party sizes: The logic of simple electoral systems.* Oxford University Press.

Taagepera, Rein, and Matthew Shugart. 1989. *Seats and votes: The effects and determinants of electoral systems.* Yale University Press.

Tavits, Margit. 2008. "The role of parties' past behavior in coalition formation." *American Political Science Review* 102.4: 495–507.

Taylor, Steven L., Matthew Soberg Shugart, Arend Lijphart, and Bernard Grofman. 2014. *A different democracy: American government in a 31-country perspective.* Yale University Press.

Thibaut, Bernhard. 1999. "Ethiopia." In Dieter Nohlen, Michael Krennerich, and Bernhard Thibaut, *Elections in Africa: A data handbook.* Oxford University Press. 373–86.

Tocqueville, Alexis de. 2001. *Democracy in America.* Penguin. Originally published in 1835.

US Department of Commerce. 1975. *Historical statistics of the United States: Colonial times to 1970.* Bicentennial ed. US Government Printing Office.

Weingast, Barry R. 1979. "A rational choice perspective on congressional norms." *American Journal of Political Science* 245–62.

Weldon, Steven, and Russell Dalton. 2014. "Democratic structures and democratic participation: The limits of consensualism theory." In Jacques Thomassen, ed., *Elections and democracy: Representation and accountability.* Oxford University Press. 113–31.

Whiteley, Paul F., and Patrick Seyd. 1999. "Discipline in the British Conservative Party: The attitudes of party activists toward the role of their Members of Parliament." In Shaun Bowler, David M. Farrell, and Richard S. Katz, eds., *Party discipline and parliamentary government.* Ohio State University Press.

Wilford, Rick, and Robin Wilson. 2003. *A route to stability: The review of the Belfast agreement.* Democratic Dialogue. August 3. Available online at https://cain. ulster.ac.uk/dd/papers/dd03agreview.pdf

Wilkinson, Steven I. 2004. *Votes and violence: Electoral competition and ethnic riots in India.* Cambridge University Press.

Wolfinger, Raymond E. 1965. "The development and persistence of ethnic voting." *American Political Science Review* 59.4: 896–908.

Zimbardo, Philip. 2007. *The Lucifer effect: Understanding how good people turn evil.* Random House.

Index